TURN TAX DEDUCTIONS INTO WEALTH

Legal Tax Strategies for W-2 Earners and Entrepreneurs

BRIAN T. BOYD, ESQ.

Turn Tax Deductions into Wealth:
Legal Tax Strategies for W-2 Earners and Entrepreneurs
by Brian T. Boyd

1. EDU013000 EDUCATION / Finance
2. LAW086000 LAW / Taxation
3. BUSINESS & ECONOMICS / Taxation / Personal *see* Personal Finance / Taxation

ISBN (paperback): 979-8-88636-077-6
ISBN (ebook): 979-8-88636-078-3

Library of Congress Control Number: 2026905524

Cover design by Lewis Agrell

Printed in the United States of America

Authority Publishing
13389 Folsom Blvd #300-256
Folsom, CA 95630
800-877-1097

www.AuthorityPublishing.com

TABLE OF CONTENTS

Preface: A Tale of Two Taxpayers v

CHAPTER 1: The New Tax Mindset—
Why Deductions Matter More Than Ever 1

CHAPTER 2: Standard Deduction—
The Simplest Tax Shelter 7

CHAPTER 3: Uncle Sam's Kickback:
The State and Local Tax (SALT) Deduction 13

CHAPTER 4: Home Sweet (Tax-Deductible) Home:
Mortgage Interest and Property Taxes 19

CHAPTER 5: Giving to Get:
The Charitable Contribution Deduction 25

CHAPTER 6: Health Is Wealth: Medical Expense
Deductions and Tax-Advantaged Health Strategies 33

CHAPTER 7: Education and Family:
Student Loan Interest, Educator Expenses,
and Other Personal Deductions 41

CHAPTER 8: No Tax on Tips:
A New Deduction for Service Workers 47

CHAPTER 9: No Tax on Overtime:
Turning Extra Hours into Extra Savings 53

CHAPTER 10: No Tax on Wheels:
The Car Loan Interest Deduction 59

CHAPTER 11: Deductions for the Side Hustle:
Ordinary and Necessary Business Expenses 65

CHAPTER 12: Home Office, Big Savings:
Turning Your Living Space into a Deduction 71

CHAPTER 13: On the Road:
Travel, Meals, and Vehicle Deductions 79

CHAPTER 14: Tools of the Trade:
Depreciation and Section 179 Expensing 83

CHAPTER 15: The 20 Percent Bonus:
The Qualified Business Income (QBI) Deduction 87

CHAPTER 16: Super-Sized Savings:
Advanced Retirement and Deferred
Compensation Strategies 91

CHAPTER 17: Real Estate Riches:
Advanced Property Tax Strategies for High Earners 95

CHAPTER 18: Investing Like the Elite:
Opportunity Zones and QSBS Strategies 99

CHAPTER 19: Strategic Giving:
Charitable Trusts, Foundations, and the
Philanthropist's Tax Playbook 103

CHAPTER 20: Entity Engineering:
S-Corps, C-Corps, and Partnerships for
High-Income Tax Planning 107

APPENDIX A: Year-Round Tax Planning Checklist. 109

APPENDIX B: Documentation and Recordkeeping Toolkit. . .113

APPENDIX C: Forms, Schedules, and Where Things Go. . . . 117

Table of Authorities 121

About The Author 123

PREFACE

౬౩౮౦

A Tale of Two Taxpayers

Meet Alex and Jordan—two friends who earn the same income but live very different financial lives. Alex is a classic W-2 employee, diligently paying taxes out of each paycheck and assuming that taxes are as inevitable as the sunrise. Jordan, on the other hand, has learned to think like an entrepreneur when it comes to taxes, even while drawing a salary. Jordan tracks expenses, devours tax books, and asks a simple question about every dollar spent: "Is there a way this could be tax-deductible?"

One evening in early 2026, over coffee, Alex vents about a small tax refund. "I barely got anything back. I guess that means I did it right—paid just enough. But I feel like I'm always behind." Jordan smiles and pulls out two tax returns from 2025—one belongs to a client who's a "poor taxpayer" (someone who misses opportunities, like Alex) and the other to a "rich taxpayer" (someone who maximizes every deduction). Both taxpayers earned $80,000 in 2025. But the poor taxpayer took the standard deduction only, while the rich taxpayer strategically claimed deductions for everything from a home office to a new law's special "overtime" deduction. The result? The rich taxpayer legally owed thousands less in taxes.

Jordan slides a simple comparison across the table. Alex's eyes widen as they read.

TABLE: Comparison of 2025 Tax Outcomes: Poor versus

Rich Taxpayer

Category—Poor Taxpayer (Alex-style) versus Rich Taxpayer (Jordan-style):

1. Gross income (same W-2 pay): $80,000 →$80,000
2. Mindset: "Taxes happen to me"→"Taxes are a system to plan within"
3. Recordkeeping: Minimal →Tracks receipts, mileage, and documentation
4. Key deductions used: Standard deduction only → Uses available deductions (e.g., qualified overtime if eligible, retirement, home office/side-hustle where applicable)
5. Credits checked: Rarely →Checks eligibility each year (education, family, energy, etc.)
6. Outcome: Higher taxable income and tax due→Lower taxable income and tax due (legally)

Comparison of 2025 tax outcomes: poor versus rich taxpayer. In the table above, both individuals earned the same salary, but the "rich taxpayer" used the rules proactively (deductions, documentation, and timing) to reduce taxable income and federal tax owed. The key takeaway is not a trick—it's planning plus proof.

"How is this possible?" Alex asks, equal parts astonished and skeptical. Jordan explains that in 2025, a new law, nicknamed the One Big Beautiful Bill Act (OBBBA), unleashed a slew of fresh tax deductions aimed at helping working Americans. "Congress essentially put some big tax breaks on the table, but you have to know they exist to grab them," Jordan says. "And even aside from the new stuff, there were already plenty of deductions people ignore. The tax code actually encourages smart financial behavior—if you pay attention."

That conversation inspired this book. In the pages to come, we follow characters like Alex (our everyman W-2 worker) and Jordan (the budding tax-savvy friend), along with entrepreneurs, teachers, and even retirees, as they navigate the world of deductions. Each chapter tackles a different type of deduction or strategy. You'll see narrative examples of how these tax rules apply in real life, charts or tables that break down the numbers, and clear explanations of the legal basis for each deduction (with footnotes pointing to the Internal Revenue Code, regulations, IRS guidance, and relevant court cases for those who love details).

By the end, you will understand how a "rich taxpayer" thinks and operates. It's not about tax evasion or any shady scheme; it's about using the incentives built into the law for your benefit. As I often tell my clients: "The tax code is thousands of pages long; somewhere in there is a gift with your name on it. Let's find it." This book will help you find your gifts. Whether you're a W-2 employee who has never itemized a deduction in your life, or a self-employed business owner juggling receipts, or even an investor or high earner looking for the next level of tax strategy—the lessons here will empower you to keep more of your hard-earned money.

So, get comfortable and maybe grab your Form 1040 for reference. As you read these chapters, imagine yourself in each story. Could you be doing the same thing to cut your taxes? Chances are, the answer is yes. The difference between paying the government and investing in your own future often boils down to knowing the rules of the game. It's time to learn those rules.

Let's begin this journey with the most important shift of all: changing how you think about taxes. As you'll see in chapter 1, a simple change in mindset—from viewing taxes as a burden to viewing them as an opportunity—can set you on the path from being a poor taxpayer to a rich taxpayer.

Note: The scenarios and individuals in this book are illustrative; however, the tax numbers and laws are very real. All tax law discussions reflect US federal income tax law as in effect in January 2026, including the One Big Beautiful Bill Act of 2025 (signed July 4, 2025) and IRS inflation adjustments for tax year 2026 where noted. Dollar thresholds can change each year; verify current-year figures for filings beyond the tax years discussed. Always consult a professional for personalized advice, but let this book serve as your comprehensive roadmap.

CHAPTER 1

ೞ

The New Tax Mindset—
Why Deductions Matter More Than Ever

"It's not how much you make, it's how much you keep."
—Robert T. Kiyosaki

Alex had heard that old adage before, but it hit differently now. In early 2025, with inflation nibbling at every dollar, Alex realized that a salary raise wasn't fully his—the IRS would take its cut off the top. Meanwhile, Alex's friend Jordan seemed to keep so much more of each dollar earned. The secret, Jordan confided, was tax deductions.

Story: Awakening to Deductions

On a chilly February morning, Alex and Jordan carpooled to work. Alex was excited about a recent pay raise to $80,000 a year. But that excitement dimmed when the first paycheck arrived and the federal withholding was higher. "I got a 10 percent raise, but my take-home only went up by maybe 7 percent. Where did the rest go?" Alex grumbled.

Jordan pulled into a parking spot and replied, "It went to taxes, of course. But have you adjusted your W-4 for the new No Tax on Overtime deduction? Or the others from that new 2025 tax law?"

Alex looked blank.

Jordan explained that the One Big Beautiful Bill Act of 2025 had created new deductions and extended others. For example, if Alex worked overtime or earned tips or even paid interest on a car loan, there were fresh deductions on the table.

Alex was surprised. "I thought deductions were just for homeowners or business owners. I'm just a single filer with a W-2."

Jordan shook his head. "That used to be kind of true, but not anymore. Lawmakers realized regular workers needed breaks too. You just have to know about them."

Deductions = Money in Your Pocket

A tax deduction reduces your taxable income. Lower taxable income means less tax, which means you keep more money. It's that simple, but the impact can be dramatic. For instance, if you're in the 22 percent tax bracket, a $1,000 deduction could save you $220 in tax. Some deductions are "above-the-line" (reducing your adjusted gross income), others are "itemized" (below-the-line, requiring you to forgo the standard deduction). We'll explore those concepts in chapter 2. What matters here is that each deduction is an opportunity to reclaim part of your paycheck from the IRS.

In 2025, deductions matter more than ever because the tax law changes gave and took away certain benefits simultaneously. The new law made the higher standard deduction permanent and even boosted it a bit, which is great for many. But it also means fewer people itemize, potentially overlooking itemizable expenses. At the same time, targeted deductions like the ones for overtime, tips, car loan interest, and seniors (all introduced in 2025) mean there are new opportunities to reduce your taxable income if you qualify. The mindset shift is to start actively looking for deductible expenses in your life.

Jordan's approach to any major spending is to ask: "Is there a tax deduction or credit for this?" When buying a car, Jordan remembered the No Tax on Car Loan Interest deduction and chose a qualifying American-assembled car, planning to deduct the interest. When choosing to pick up extra shifts, Jordan knew the overtime premium portion could be deducted under the new law. These decisions illustrate the proactive mindset of a "rich taxpayer."

The 2025 Law: A Big (Beautiful) Deal

Let's briefly outline what the One Big Beautiful Bill Act of 2025 (OBBBA) changed for individual taxpayers, because it set the stage for many chapters in this book. This massive law (Public Law 119-21) was signed on July 4, 2025. It did a lot, but here are key points that a savvy taxpayer should know:

- Extended tax cuts: It permanently extended the lower tax brackets from the 2017 Tax Cuts and Jobs Act (TCJA) so the rates on your income didn't jump back up in 2026 as they were scheduled to. In fact, it even tweaked brackets to be a bit more generous at the low end.
- Higher standard deduction: It locked in the doubled standard deduction from TCJA and nudged it slightly higher for 2025 ($15,750 single, $31,500 married). That's a simple deduction anyone can take.
- New deductions for workers: It created four temporary deductions for 2025 to 2028: "No Tax on Tips," "No Tax on Overtime," "No Tax on Car Loan Interest," and an extra deduction for seniors over sixty-five years old. These are targeted at middle-class folks—service industry employees, hourly workers, car-buyers, and retirees.
- SALT cap raised: It raised the cap on the state and local tax (SALT) deduction from $10,000 to $40,000 for 2025 to 2029, but with a twist: If your income is over $500,000, that cap starts to shrink back down. So higher earners get less benefit from SALT. (We'll unpack this in chapter 3.)
- Permanent rules: It made permanent many TCJA

changes that were due to expire after 2025: the lower mortgage interest cap ($750,000 of debt); no more miscellaneous itemized deductions like unreimbursed job expenses (except a new carve-out for educators); and no return of the Pease itemized deduction phase-out. In short, the tax landscape of 2018 to 2025 is largely the new normal going forward.

- New "Trump Accounts" for kids: The law even created new tax-advantaged savings accounts nicknamed "Trump Accounts" for children—interesting, but not a deduction. (It's more like a new type of IRA for minors.) I mention it in case you hear the term.

By the end of 2025, the IRS was busy issuing guidance on how to claim the new deductions. Tax pros and news sites were buzzing. Yet many everyday taxpayers like Alex might have missed the memo. This book is here to make sure you don't miss out.

Mindset in Action: A Quick Example

Consider two coworkers, each earning $60,000 in 2025 with a little side income. Both rent their homes (no mortgage interest deduction) and have moderate state taxes. Chris, the "poor taxpayer," takes the standard deduction of $15,750 and calls it a day, figuring there's nothing else to do. Pat, the "rich taxpayer" mindset coworker, takes the standard deduction and also claims $5,000 in overtime pay deduction (Pat picked up extra shifts), and $2,000 in student loan interest paid, and maxes out a retirement account at work which isn't a deduction on the return but lowers taxable wages. Pat also kept track of an unreimbursed $300 work expense—not normally deductible under TCJA rules, but since Pat is a teacher, it's fully deductible as an itemized expense beyond the standard deduction due to the new carve-out (we'll discuss that in chapter 7).

At tax time, Chris has taxable income of roughly $44,250

(after the $15,750 standard deduction). Pat, on the other hand, has taxable income closer to $37,250 after factoring in those above-the-line deductions and adjustments. Assuming a 22 percent marginal bracket for simplicity, Pat will owe roughly $1,540 less in federal tax than Chris. That's real money saved.

Now, $1,500 might not sound life-changing, but remember: Pat didn't earn extra money—Pat simply kept more of what was earned. Over a decade, if such differences persist, the one who consistently maximizes deductions could be tens of thousands of dollars ahead. Those savings can seed an investment account, pay down debt, or fund further education.

As the numbers show, Pat's deductions and adjustments reduce taxable income by roughly $7,000 versus Chris—about $1,500 of federal tax savings at a 22 percent marginal rate.

- Taxable income comparison—Chris versus Pat: With the same gross income, Pat's proactive use of deductions and adjustments lowers taxable income significantly compared to Chris, illustrating the power of a tax-aware mindset. Pat's example demonstrates the mindset shift: Even as a W-2 earner, Pat thought like an entrepreneur about deductions.

Chapter 1 Key Takeaway:

- Begin viewing every major life or financial event through a tax lens. If you get a bonus or work overtime—think deduction. If you go back to school—think Lifetime Learning credit or tuition deduction. If you support an elderly parent—think about the dependent credit or medical deductions. This book will give you the tools to connect those dots.

Before we dive into specific deductions in the coming chapters, here's a quick roadmap of what's ahead: Chapter 2 will ensure you understand the difference between taking the standard deduction and itemizing and how the new 2025 rules affect that choice. Chapters 3 through 7 will cover the classic itemized deductions (SALT, mortgage interest, charity, medical, etc.) and some adjustments like student loan interest and educator expenses. Chapters 8 through 10 will explain the brand-new deductions from OBBBA (tips, overtime, car loan interest, seniors). Chapters 11 through 15 focus on deductions especially relevant to self-employed folks and small business owners (home office, business expenses, depreciation, and the 20 percent Qualified Business Income deduction).

Then, for those hungry for more, chapters 16 through 20 step up to advanced strategies for higher earners (think six-figure incomes and above). That includes maximizing retirement vehicles, real estate tricks for big tax write-offs, charitable giving strategies of the wealthy, and choosing the right business entity for tax efficiency. Even if you're not there yet income-wise, peeking into those strategies can inspire your journey (and if you are there, get ready to take notes!).

So, with the groundwork laid and your mindset primed, let's turn the page to chapter 2 and talk about the foundational choice every taxpayer faces each year: standard deduction or itemize? Get this right, and you're on your way to being a rich taxpayer.

CHAPTER 2

cଷ∞

Standard Deduction—
The Simplest Tax Shelter

Alex sat at the kitchen table, a shoebox of receipts in hand, frowning at a checklist of potential deductions: medical bills, charitable donations, property taxes, etc. The year was 2025, and Alex remembered Jordan's advice to always compare taking the standard deduction versus itemizing. "The standard deduction is basically a freebie, but itemizing could save more if your expenses are high enough," Jordan had said. With the recent law changes, Alex wasn't sure what the right move was this time.

The Basics of the Standard Deduction

The standard deduction is a fixed dollar amount that almost every taxpayer can subtract from their income, no questions asked. It's the IRS's way of giving you some tax-free income without needing proof of expenses. For 2025, the standard deduction amounts (thanks to OBBBA's slight increase) are: $15,750 for single filers; $31,500 for married filing jointly; and $23,625 for heads of household. These amounts will adjust slightly each year for inflation. If you're sixty-five or older, or you're blind, you get an additional standard deduction on top. (In 2025 it's $1,950 extra for singles or heads of household; $1,500 each if married.)

For most folks, the standard deduction is the simplest and often the best choice. In fact, after the 2017 tax reform nearly doubled these amounts, the percentage of people itemizing deductions plummeted—from about 31 percent in 2017 to roughly 8 percent in 2022. OBBBA cemented those higher amounts permanently, so the era of fewer itemizers is here to stay.

Think of the standard deduction as a built-in tax shelter that requires zero effort. If your allowable expenses—like mortgage interest, state taxes, charitable gifts, etc.—don't exceed the standard deduction, you simply claim the standard amount and effectively shield that portion of your income from tax. It's like an automatic tax credit for just existing.

2025 Changes: A Boost and a Bonus for Seniors

What's new in 2025? The standard deduction got a boost (those odd numbers above reflect a 5 percent bump Congress provided). Also, OBBBA introduced a Temporary Deduction for Seniors: If you or your spouse are sixty-five or older, you can claim an additional $6,000 deduction per senior from 2025 to 2028. This is on top of the normal extra $1,950 for ages sixty-five and older. It's essentially Congress giving seniors a double dip because personal exemptions were eliminated back in 2018. The senior deduction does start to phase out at higher incomes ($75,000 single or $150,000 joint), but for middle-class retirees, it's a big deal. We'll illustrate this in a moment.

Example: Meet Sam and Pat, a married couple both sixty-six years old, filing jointly in 2025 (MFJ). They rent their home and have modest itemizable expenses, say $5,000 of medical over the threshold and $3,000 of charity—nowhere near the normal standard deduction. Normally, they'd just take the $31,500 standard. But now, being over sixty-five, they each qualify for the new $6,000 senior deduction, plus the regular age bonus. So their total deduction is: $31,500 (base standard for MFJ) + $12,000 (two seniors × $6,000) + $3,000 (two seniors × $150,000 regular extra) = $46,500! This means their first $46,500 of income is tax-free. If their combined income was, say, $60,000 (perhaps from Social Security and a part-time job), their taxable income would only be $13,500. At a 10 to 12 percent tax rate, that's practically no tax due.

- Impact of the Senior Deduction: In the example above, the senior couple's taxable income is dramatically lower than a non-senior couple with the same $60,000 income because of the additional $12,000 senior deduction (on top of the standard deduction). That difference can reduce federal tax from "a few thousand" to only a few hundred dollars, depending on brackets.

This new senior deduction is found in IRC § 151(d)(5) as amended (technically, it's an "additional exemption amount" but functions like a deduction). It's temporary, though—unless extended, it's only for 2025 through 2028.

Standard versus Itemized: When to Itemize

How do you decide whether to stick with standard or to itemize? The rule of thumb is: itemize if your allowable personal deductions exceed the standard deduction for your filing status. Allowable itemized deductions include things like:

- State and local taxes (income or sales, plus property taxes)—capped at $40,000 through 2029 per OBBBA, and potentially less if high income (chapter 3 will detail this).
- Home mortgage interest (on loans up to $750,000, or $1 million if an older loan).
- Charitable contributions (with limits, usually 60

percent of adjusted gross income, or AGI, for cash to public charities).

- Medical expenses beyond 7.5 percent of AGI.
- A few others (casualty losses in disasters, etc.—and now educator expenses if you're a teacher buying school supplies).

If the sum of those exceeds your standard amount, itemizing will reduce your taxable income more than the standard deduction would. If not, take the standard.

Example: Alex's shoebox of receipts includes $8,000 of state taxes, $5,000 of charitable donations, and $2,000 of out-of-pocket medical expenses above the 7.5 percent AGI threshold. Plus, Alex paid $1,000 interest on a car loan (a new thing Alex heard might be deductible). For a single filer, these itemized would sum to $8,000 + $5,000 + $2,000 = $15,000 (the car loan interest deduction we will discuss in chapter 10 actually counts as an adjustment separate from itemized, so keep it aside for now). Compared to the standard $15,750, itemizing yields $750 less deduction—not worth it. Alex should just take the $15,750 standard (and separately claim the car interest above-the-line deduction).

However, consider Jordan, who owns a home. Jordan's 2025 itemizables: $10,000 SALT (maxed out) + $12,000 mortgage interest + $3,000 charity = $25,000, clearly above the $15,750 standard. Jordan should itemize and deduct $25,000. Jordan benefits from itemizing by an extra ~$9,250 deduction beyond the standard. In a 22 percent bracket, that's about a $2,000 tax saved.

It's always worthwhile to run the numbers both ways (most tax software does this automatically). Note that even if you don't have enough to itemize federally, some states with income tax have lower standard deductions, so you might itemize on the state return.

The "Zero Tax" Phenomenon

One thing the beefed-up standard deduction did is remove many lower-income folks from the tax rolls entirely. If your income is below the standard deduction (plus any senior add-ons), you owe $0 tax because your taxable income is zero or negative. For instance, an unmarried retiree over sixty-five in 2025 could have income up to around $21,750 (standard $15,750 + senior $6,000) and owe nothing in federal tax. That's intentional—Congress wanted to shield low incomes.

For planning, if you're nearing retirement or in between jobs with a lower income year, the standard deduction can cover a lot. Those might be good years to do things like convert a traditional IRA to a Roth up to the deduction limit (so you pay no tax on the conversion—an advanced move, which we'll discuss more of in chapter 17).

Above-the-Line Deductions and the Standard Deduction

One great feature of the new worker-focused deductions (tips, overtime, and car loan interest) and other "adjustments" (like IRA contributions, student loan interest, HSA contributions, self-employed health insurance—see upcoming chapters) is that you can claim them even if you take the standard deduction. They are not itemized deductions; they either come off your gross income in arriving at AGI or as special line deductions. OBBBA explicitly made the tips and overtime deductions available to "both itemizing and non-itemizing taxpayers." So don't think that taking the standard deduction means you can't also benefit from those above-the-line breaks.

Alex, for example, will likely take the standard deduction, but can still claim the overtime deduction from chapter 9, the student loan interest deduction from chapter 7, etc., above the line. Those will further reduce taxable income beyond the standard amount.

Quick Tip: Married versus Separate

- A quick note for married folks: If you're married filing jointly, you get that big $31,500 standard (2025). If you file separately, you each get $15,750 but if one spouse itemizes, the other must also itemize (even if it's not beneficial). So usually married couples either both standard or both itemize. Jointly is usually better unless there's a special situation (like huge medical bills on one spouse's income).

Chapter Summary

The standard deduction is your baseline. It's easy, it's generous, and for many, it's the best option. But always check if you might do better by itemizing. The effort of gathering receipts is worth it if it saves you hundreds or thousands in tax. In our rich taxpayer versus poor taxpayer theme: the poor taxpayer blindly takes the standard deduction without considering itemizing (or vice versa, itemizes out of habit even when it's not beneficial). The rich taxpayer runs the numbers both ways and makes an informed choice every year.

In chapter 3, we will dive into the most common (and often the largest) category of itemized deductions: state and local taxes, a.k.a. SALT. You'll learn how the new $40,000 cap works and why, in high-tax states, even the well-off might not get to deduct as much as they'd like. Understanding SALT will further clarify whether itemizing is in the cards for you.

CHAPTER 3

CʒʒƆ

Uncle Sam's Kickback:
The State and Local Tax (SALT) Deduction

Alex never enjoyed looking at paystubs, mostly because the state income tax line felt like a rude surprise every two weeks. Property taxes were something Alex only heard about from homeowners—burdensome, mysterious, and seemingly unavoidable. But one evening, while Alex and Jordan reviewed last year's return at the kitchen table, Jordan tapped a line item Alex had always overlooked.

"You've been paying this tax your whole life," Jordan said. "But have you ever used it to your advantage?"

Alex looked confused. "You mean income tax?"

Jordan shook his head. "I mean the state and local tax deduction—SALT. You've been paying into the system without ever claiming your refund on the back end."

A Hidden Deduction in Plain Sight

Jordan explained that the Internal Revenue Code allows taxpayers who itemize to deduct certain taxes they pay to state and local governments—taxes they were going to pay anyway. The idea is simple: Congress recognized that taxpayers should not be taxed twice on the same money, first by the state and then by the federal government. The deduction, found in IRC §164, includes three major components:

- state and local income taxes
- real property taxes
- personal property taxes based on value

Alex sipped a cup of coffee and stared at the list. "So you're telling me I've been paying deductible taxes for years and just… never deducted them?"

Jordan smiled. "You and millions of others."

How the SALT Deduction Works

For decades, the SALT deduction had no meaningful limit. High-income taxpayers in high-tax states benefited tremendously. But everything changed in 2017 when Congress capped the deduction at $10,000 per tax return. That cap remained in place until the One Big Beautiful Bill Act of 2025 (OBBBA) dramatically reshaped the landscape.

Jordan leaned back. "Congress realized the cap was squeezing middle-class taxpayers in high-tax states, not just the wealthy. So in 2025, they raised the cap to $40,000."

Alex nearly choked on the coffee. "From ten to forty? That's a massive change!"

"It is," Jordan replied. "At least for some people."

Under the 2025 law, the SALT deduction cap increased to $40,000 per return—but with an income-based twist. The full cap applies only until a taxpayer reaches certain income thresholds. Once income rises too high, the SALT deduction begins to phase down, though it never falls below $10,000.

For tax year 2026, the cap increases to $40,400, and the phase-down threshold rises to $505,000 (both indexed for inflation).

The message was clear: Congress wanted the expanded deduction to help middle-class taxpayers, not exclusively high-income individuals.

What Counts toward the SALT Deduction

Jordan grabbed a scratchpad and wrote three simple categories:

1. State Income Taxes

Almost every W-2 employee pays state income tax through payroll withholding. These amounts are deductible to the extent they fall within the SALT cap.

2. Real Estate Property Taxes
Homeowners can deduct real estate taxes they pay on a primary residence, second home, or land they own. Renters cannot deduct property taxes directly, though such taxes may influence rental rates.

3. Sales Taxes (as an Alternative)
In states without an income tax—like Florida, Texas, Tennessee, and Washington—taxpayers may instead deduct state and local sales taxes. The IRS even publishes optional sales tax tables for taxpayers who do not wish to keep all receipts.

Alex blinked. "So I get to choose between deducting income taxes or sales taxes?"

"Yes," Jordan answered. "Whichever is higher."

Two Taxpayers, Two Very Different Outcomes

Jordan offered a tale of two married couples—Taylor and Morgan—to illustrate how dramatically the SALT deduction can differ depending on income.

Taylor: Middle-Class Homeowners
- o   Married filing jointly
- o   Income: $140,000
- o   State taxes: $5,500
- o   Property taxes: $11,000
- o   Total SALT: $16,500

Under the new law, Taylor can deduct the full $16,500, making itemizing potentially worthwhile.

Morgan: High-Income Taxpayers
- o   Married filing jointly
- o   Income: $650,000
- o   State taxes: $25,000
- o   Property taxes: $18,000
- o   Total SALT: $43,000

While Taylor benefits fully, Morgan does not. Because Morgan's income exceeds $500,000, the SALT cap is reduced by 30 percent of the amount above $500,000. At $650,000 of income, the reduction is 30 percent x $150,000 = $45,000, which pushes the cap down to the $10,000 minimum. So even though Morgan paid $43,000 in state and local taxes, the federal SALT deduction is limited to $10,000.

Alex frowned. "Same taxes. Same house. But the wealthier couple gets less of a deduction?"

Jordan nodded. "That's the design. Congress expanded the benefit, but only up to a point."

When Does SALT Make Itemizing Worth It?

Alex learned that for many taxpayers—especially homeowners—the SALT deduction is often the single largest itemized expense. Consider a taxpayer who pays:

- $6,000 state income tax; and
- $4,000 property tax.

The total SALT amount of $10,000 already approaches the standard deduction for many single taxpayers. If the taxpayer also has mortgage interest or charitable contributions, itemizing becomes not only sensible but potentially advantageous.

"Think of SALT as a foundation," Jordan said. "If your SALT number is high enough, it becomes the anchor for itemizing."

Common Misunderstandings About SALT

Jordan clarified mistakes that frequently cause taxpayers to overclaim or underclaim the deduction:

- **X** HOA fees: Not deductible. These are association dues, not taxes.
- **X** Government service fees: Sewer, trash collection, and inspection fees do not qualify unless they are based on the value of property.
- **X** Federal taxes: Not deductible under any circumstance.

SALT and the Alternative Minimum Tax (AMT)

Alex had once received a letter mentioning AMT and never wanted to relive the experience.

"If nothing else," Alex asked, "does AMT mess with SALT?"

Jordan answered without hesitation, "Yes. SALT is not deductible at all when calculating AMT."

Fortunately, far fewer taxpayers face AMT after the reforms of 2017 and 2025. Still, high-income taxpayers must remain aware of AMT interaction before banking on the SALT deduction.

Advanced SALT Strategy: Pass-Through Entity Workaround

Jordan leaned in, lowering his voice, as if sharing a secret. "There's a workaround for business owners that the IRS explicitly approved. It's huge."

Many states now allow partnerships and S corporations to pay state income taxes at the entity level. Because business-level taxes are deductible without regard to the SALT cap, owners of these entities get the benefit indirectly. This method—known as the PTE tax election—has been a powerful planning tool for high-income individuals.

"The IRS blessed it," Jordan added, "so it's perfectly legitimate."

Alex Starts to See the Bigger Picture

Alex pulled out a notepad and began jotting down numbers:
- Income: $92,000
- State income tax: $4,750
- New property taxes: $7,200
- Total SALT: $11,950

For the first time ever, Alex realized there might be enough deductions to justify itemizing.

"I always thought itemizing was for rich people," Alex said.

Jordan shook his head. "It's for anyone who pays attention."

Chapter Summary

By the end of the night, Alex understood what Jordan had been trying to teach since Chapter 1.

Key lessons:

- Many taxes you pay are potential deductions, not sunk costs.
- The 2025 increase in the SALT cap significantly benefits middle-income taxpayers.
- Itemizing is worthwhile when SALT and other deductions exceed the standard deduction.
- High-income taxpayers must contend with phase-outs and AMT limits.
- Business owners may access special workarounds unavailable to W-2 employees.

As Alex packed up the notepad, there was a newfound confidence in the air. The lesson was clear:

A rich taxpayer sees a deduction where a poor taxpayer sees only a bill.

CHAPTER 4

ଓଃଇ

Home Sweet (Tax-Deductible) Home: Mortgage Interest and Property Taxes

Alex had always dreamed of owning a home. Not a mansion or a penthouse—just something modest with a quiet home office and a backyard big enough for weekend barbecues. When Alex finally signed the mortgage paperwork on a small two-bedroom townhouse, the excitement was overwhelming. That is, until the first mortgage statement arrived, showing a line item Alex had never considered deeply: interest.

"So most of my payment isn't even going toward the loan balance yet?" Alex asked Jordan one afternoon, waving the mortgage statement like a white flag.

Jordan grinned. "Welcome to homeownership. And congratulations—you've just opened the door to one of the biggest tax deductions available to everyday Americans."

Alex raised a brow. "You mean… this interest is deductible?"

"You better believe it," Jordan said. "And that's one of the main reasons the tax code still strongly encourages buying a home."

The Mortgage Interest Deduction: A Timeless Benefit with Modern Limits

Jordan explained that the mortgage interest deduction allows homeowners to deduct interest paid on loans used to buy, build, or improve their homes. For decades, the deduction was one of the pillars of the middle class, making homeownership more affordable.

But tax laws have changed.

Before 2017, taxpayers could deduct interest on mortgage balances up to $1 million. After the Tax Cuts and Jobs Act (TCJA), that limit dropped to $750,000 for loans originated after December 15, 2017. The One Big Beautiful Bill Act (OBBBA) of 2025 made this limit permanent.

"So if I have a mortgage under $750,000," Alex asked, "I can deduct all the interest I pay?"

"Exactly," Jordan replied. "And you're nowhere near the limit with your townhouse, so you get the full benefit."

The deduction only applies if a taxpayer itemizes, but for many homeowners—especially in combination with property taxes and others—itemizing becomes the better deal.

Qualified Residence Interest: What the IRS Actually Allows

Jordan pointed to two categories of deductible mortgage interest:

- Acquisition indebtedness—debt used to buy, build, or substantially improve a qualified residence.
- Home equity indebtedness—historically deductible; but beginning in 2018, only deductible if used for acquisition or improvement.

"People get this wrong all the time," Jordan added. "You can't deduct interest from a home equity loan you used to pay off credit cards or take a vacation. It has to relate to improving the home."

Alex nodded, making mental notes.

Example: Alex's First Year of Homeownership

Jordan ran through a practical illustration:

- Loan amount: $310,000
- First-year mortgage interest paid: $10,800
- Property taxes: $7,200

"If you itemize," Jordan said, "your mortgage interest and property taxes alone give you $18,000 in deductions. Add in charitable giving or state taxes, and you'll almost certainly surpass the standard deduction."

For the first time, Alex realized owning a home wasn't just an emotional milestone—it was a strategic tax move.

Property Taxes: The Second Half of the Equation

Alex had always believed property taxes were nothing but a financial burden.

Jordan countered: "Property taxes can be a blessing at tax time. They count toward your itemized deductions under the SALT umbrella, and thanks to the 2025 law, the SALT cap is much more generous."

Jordan reminded Alex that before 2025, the SALT deduction (which includes state income or sales tax, plus property tax) was capped at $10,000. After OBBBA, the cap rose to $40,000, giving homeowners far more room to deduct their taxes—though with phaseouts at higher income levels.

"Your $7,200 in property taxes fits comfortably," Jordan said. "It counts fully—unless your income skyrockets above the phaseout thresholds."

Alex laughed. "One thing at a time."

What Counts as Real Property Tax?

Jordan listed the requirements:

- It must be a tax, not a fee.
- It must be imposed at the state or local level.
- It must be based on the assessed value of the property.

"People try to deduct utility fees, trash pickup, or HOA dues," Jordan explained. "But none of those qualify. They're not considered real property taxes under the tax code."

Alex noted that the tax law is very particular, and precision matters.

When Mortgage Interest Isn't Deductible

Jordan stressed that not all home-related interest qualifies. Common mistakes include:

1. Excess Loan Amounts
Interest on mortgage debt above $750,000 (for loans originated after 2017) is not deductible.

2. Home Equity Loans for Non-Home Purposes
If Alex borrowed $20,000 on a home equity line to buy a car or pay off a credit card, the interest would not be deductible.

3. Personal Use Property
Vacation homes may qualify, but only if the taxpayer meets specific use requirements. A property rented out too often may no longer be treated as a residence for interest-deduction purposes.

Jordan chuckled. "There's always fine print in tax law."

Interest on Points and PMI

Alex had heard about "points" paid at closing but wasn't sure what they were. Jordan clarified:

Points (prepaid interest) may be deductible in the year paid under certain conditions.

Private mortgage insurance (PMI) may also be deductible, though it is subject to income-based phaseouts.

"Congress has played ping-pong with PMI deductibility," Jordan said. "Sometimes it's allowed, sometimes not. In 2025, we're in a window where you still get the deduction."

Alex smirked. "So we just enjoy it while it lasts?"

"Exactly."

The Psychological Shift: Seeing the Home as an Asset and a Tax Tool

Jordan leaned forward. "You're not just paying a mortgage—you're paying yourself in deductions, equity, and long-term financial stability."

The mortgage interest deduction cushions the early years of homeownership, when interest costs are highest. Property taxes remain deductible up to the SALT cap. Together, these can dramatically reduce taxable income.

Alex felt a sense of empowerment.

"It's like the tax code is quietly cheering me on for buying a home."

"More like nudging you toward stability," Jordan corrected. "Congress incentivizes homeownership because people who own homes tend to build wealth, and wealthier people are less financially vulnerable."

Alex thought about this. "So homeownership is basically a partnership—me and the IRS?"

"That's one way to visualize it," Jordan replied. "At least while the deductions last."

Preparing for the Future: When to Reevaluate

Jordan cautioned Alex:

"Don't forget that tax law changes. While OBBBA made some mortgage rules permanent, Congress can always rewrite the rules."

Alex asked, "How often should I reevaluate whether itemizing makes sense?"

"Every year," Jordan said. "Your income, mortgage interest, property taxes, and charitable deductions all change annually. Being a rich taxpayer means paying attention."

Chapter Summary

By the time they closed their notebooks, Alex saw the home—and the tax return—in an entirely new light.

Key lessons:

- Mortgage interest is often one of the largest deductions for new homeowners.

- Property taxes are fully deductible up to the SALT cap.
- Not all interest qualifies—only acquisition-related debt within specific limits.
- Itemizing may become the better choice once homeownership begins.
- Tax deductions transform homeownership into a strategic financial tool.

Alex leaned back in the chair, smiling.

"I used to think buying a home meant burying myself in debt," Alex said. "Now it feels like I've opened a door."

Jordan grinned.

"You have. And on the other side of that door is a tax return that finally starts working for you."

CHAPTER 5

ೞ

Giving to Get:
The Charitable Contribution Deduction

The December air carried a chill as Alex walked downtown past the holiday lights. At the corner, near a small coffee shop, a local charity had set up a booth collecting winter coats for families in need. Alex dropped off two gently used jackets and felt a warm wave of satisfaction. But as Alex walked away, Jordan—ever the tax strategist—appeared with a familiar half-smile.

"Good feeling, right?" Jordan asked.

Alex nodded. "Yeah. Honestly, I didn't think about taxes at all this time."

Jordan tilted his head. "Well, the good news is you can think about both. Charity helps others—but it can help you too."

Alex laughed. "Let me guess: tax deductions?"

Jordan winked. "Exactly."

Charitable Giving: Where Heart Meets Strategy

Few deductions are as emotionally satisfying as charitable contributions. Unlike taxes or mortgage interest, giving feels empowering. The tax code recognizes this and rewards generosity under Internal Revenue Code §170, allowing taxpayers to deduct contributions made to qualified charitable organizations.

"That's the key word," Jordan emphasized. *"Qualified."*

Alex raised a brow. "So not every donation counts?"

"Right. Giving twenty bucks to your neighbor doesn't count—no matter how much they need it."

What Qualifies as a Deductible Contribution?

Jordan explained that deductible contributions must be made to organizations the IRS formally recognizes as charities, such as:

- 501(c)(3) public charities;
- churches and religious organizations;
- educational institutions;
- certain nonprofit hospitals; and
- governmental entities for public purposes.

"Basically," Jordan said, "anything the IRS sees as serving a public good."

The donation can be:

- cash;
- property (clothes, furniture, vehicles, artwork);
- securities (stocks and bonds); or
- real estate.

But each category has its own rules.

The Receipt Rule

Alex's face fell. "So, about those jackets… do I need a receipt?"

Jordan nodded. "Yup. Contributions must be substantiated to be deductible, even non-cash items."

Alex reached into a pocket and found a small slip—luckily obtained from the volunteer at the booth.

Jordan continued:

- For cash gifts, a bank record or written acknowledgment is required.
- For non-cash gifts over $500, Form 8283 must be

completed.

- For gifts over $5,000, a qualified appraisal is required.

Alex blinked. "So the bigger the donation, the more paperwork?"

"Pretty much," Jordan said.

The AGI Limits: How Much Can You Deduct?

Jordan began sketching numbers.

The tax code limits charitable deductions to a percentage of a taxpayer's adjusted gross income (AGI):

- Cash contributions to public charities: up to 60 percent of AGI.
- Donations of appreciated property: generally 30 percent of AGI.
- Gifts to private foundations: 20 percent or 30 percent, depending on type.

"Most people never hit the limits," Jordan said. "But higher-income taxpayers need to plan ahead."

Alex nodded slowly. "So I can't just donate a million dollars and deduct it all if I only earn a hundred thousand?"

"Exactly. The IRS doesn't let you wipe out your income entirely through charity."

Cash Donations: Simple and Powerful

Jordan explained that cash contributions are the most straightforward. If Alex donates $2,000 in cash to a qualified charity during the year, he can deduct the full $2,000—assuming he itemizes.

Alex smiled. "That's easy."

Jordan leaned in. "Want to make it more powerful? Donate appreciated stock instead of cash."

Donating Appreciated Assets: A Hidden Gem

"Why would I give away stock?" Alex asked.

"Because it's a tax triple-play," Jordan answered.

Alex avoids paying capital gains tax on the appreciated value. He gets a deduction for the full fair market value of the stock. And the charity pays no tax when it sells the stock.

Jordan gave an example:

- Alex bought stock for $1,000 years ago.
- It's now worth $5,000.
- Alex donates the stock directly to charity.

"You just avoided tax on a $4,000 gain and got a $5,000 deduction," Jordan said.

Alex's eyes widened. "That's… incredible."

Jordan nodded. "This is how wealthy people do philanthropy. They give assets—not cash."

Non-Cash Donations: Clothing, Furniture, and Household Items

Alex thought of the winter coats donated earlier.

"These things count too," Jordan said. "But you deduct the fair market value, not the original price."

The IRS expects reasonable valuation:

- A $200 jacket might now be worth $40.
- A used sofa might be valued at $75.

"If you donate a car," Jordan added, "the rules get more complicated. The deduction usually depends on what the charity does with the vehicle."

Alex wrote a reminder: "Check IRS rules before donating big items."

Charitable Mileage and Out-of-Pocket Expenses

Jordan explained another overlooked deduction: mileage and expenses incurred while doing charitable work.

Driving to volunteer events.

Buying supplies used strictly for charity.

Expenses incurred on behalf of the organization.

The mileage deduction is modest, but it adds up for frequent volunteers.

Alex laughed. "I didn't know even my miles could be charitable."

When Charity Doesn't Count

Jordan also warned Alex about mistakes that disqualify contributions:

1. Quid Pro Quo Donations
If Alex received something of value (like a dinner, concert ticket, or merchandise), only the excess of payment over fair market value is deductible.

2. Donations to Individuals
Charitable intent doesn't equal a charitable deduction.

3. Political Contributions
Completely non-deductible.

Alex sighed. "So buying a $500 gala ticket only gets me a deduction if the dinner is worth less than $500?"

Jordan nodded. "Right. If the meal is valued at $120, then $380 is deductible."

A Story of Two Taxpayers: Chris and Bailey

Jordan illustrated the difference between the poor taxpayer mindset and the rich taxpayer mindset using two coworkers—Chris and Bailey—who each donated $1,000 during the year.

Chris: The Poor Taxpayer

Chris wrote several $100 checks to different charities, never asked for receipts, and tossed most records. At tax time, Chris had no documentation and couldn't substantiate donations. Result: No deduction.

Bailey: The Rich Taxpayer

Bailey donated appreciated stock worth $1,000 but purchased for $300

Avoided capital gains tax, obtained written acknowledgment from the charity, and itemized deductions

Result: Bailey deducted the full $1,000 and saved hundreds in tax.

Alex shook his head. "So recordkeeping really is the difference between a tax deduction and nothing."

Jordan smiled. "Always."

Charitable Bunching: A Strategy for Itemizers

As the conversation deepened, Jordan described the concept of bunching.

Because the standard deduction is so high in 2025, many taxpayers do not itemize every year. But with bunching, Alex could:

- make two or three years' worth of charitable gifts in one calendar year;
- itemize that high-deduction year; and
- take the standard deduction in the next year or two.

2026 Update: A Charitable Deduction Even If You Don't Itemize

Starting in 2026, taxpayers who take the standard deduction can also claim a separate above-the-line charitable deduction for cash gifts to qualifying public charities: up to $1,000 (single) or $2,000 (married filing jointly). This is in addition to the standard deduction and is generally not available for gifts to donor-advised funds or certain private foundations.

Also starting in 2026, individuals who itemize face a new 0.5 percent floor for charitable deductions: only the portion of otherwise-allowable charitable contributions that exceeds 0.5 percent of your contribution base (generally AGI) counts as an itemized deduction. Example: If your AGI is $200,000, the first $1,000 of itemized giving produces no charitable deduction; amounts above that threshold may be deductible (subject to the usual AGI limits).

Note: This floor can make "bunching" even more valuable—timing gifts so they clear the floor in a single year may increase the tax benefit.

"This," Jordan said, "is how you turn generosity into tax strategy."

Alex liked the idea. "So essentially, I'm timing the giving to maximize tax benefit."

"Exactly."

The Wealthy's Secret Weapon: Donor-Advised Funds

Jordan explained one last tool—the donor-advised fund (DAF).

A DAF allows the taxpayer to:

- contribute a large sum today;
- receive the full deduction in the current year; and
- distribute the funds to charities gradually over many years.

"To the IRS," Jordan said, "it's charity. To you, it's tax planning."

Alex scribbled another note: "Research DAFs."

Chapter Summary

By the end of the conversation, Alex understood why charitable giving is a favorite tool of both everyday taxpayers and wealthy individuals.

Key lessons:

- Charitable gifts reduce taxable income.
- Different types of gifts carry different tax advantages.
- Proper documentation is essential.
- Appreciated property can yield outsized tax savings.
- Bunching and donor-advised funds can increase deductions strategically.

Alex walked past the coat donation booth again that evening, smiling to the volunteers.

Helping others warmed Alex's heart.

Now, Alex knew it could also warm the tax return.

CHAPTER 6

೮೩೮೦

Health Is Wealth: Medical Expense Deductions and Tax-Advantaged Health Strategies

Alex sat in the waiting room of a small clinic, flipping through a magazine while waiting for an annual check-up. The rising cost of healthcare weighed heavily on Alex's mind. Every year seemed more expensive—premiums, copays, prescriptions, even surprise bills for lab work. Later that week, Alex vented to Jordan over lunch.

"I feel like I'm paying more for healthcare than for groceries," Alex said. "Is any of it deductible?"

Jordan smiled knowingly. "Some of it, yes. But the rules are more complicated than people think."

Alex leaned in. "Complicated how?"

"Complicated enough," Jordan said, "that most taxpayers leave money on the table without realizing it."

That was the start of Alex's journey into understanding the medical expense deduction.

The Medical Expense Deduction: A High Hurdle with Big Potential

Jordan explained that taxpayers who itemize can deduct unreimbursed medical expenses that exceed 7.5 percent of their adjusted gross income (AGI).

"So if I make $80,000 a year," Alex said, thinking aloud, "then 7.5 percent is…"

"Six thousand dollars," Jordan finished. "Exactly. Only the expenses above that amount count."

Alex sighed. "That seems impossible."

"It feels impossible until something big happens," Jordan said. "A surgery. Dental implants. Long-term care. Family medical issues. When it rains, it pours. And when it pours, the deduction suddenly matters."

Alex nodded slowly. "I guess medical costs can add up fast."

What Medical Expenses Are Deductible?

Jordan pulled out a notepad and began listing items.

"Here's what the IRS considers deductible medical expenses," Jordan said:

- Doctor and hospital fees
- Prescription medications
- Dental work (including braces)
- Glasses and contacts
- Medical equipment
- Hearing aids
- Mental health counseling
- Health insurance premiums (in limited cases)
- Long-term care services and eligible insurance premiums
- Transportation for medical care
- Certain home modifications for medical necessity

Alex blinked. "Wait—transportation?"

"Yes," Jordan replied. "If you drive to a specialist an hour away, that mileage may count."

"Even parking fees?"

"Yup. As long as the trip was primarily for medical care."

Alex wrote that down carefully.

What Doesn't Count

Jordan followed with a list of non-deductible items:

- Over-the-counter medications (unless prescribed)
- Cosmetic surgery (unless correcting a deformity or illness)
- Gym memberships
- Vitamins (except prescribed therapeutic doses)
- Health foods
- Non-prescription supplements

"Basically," Jordan said with a smirk, "healthy living isn't deductible unless a doctor explicitly tells you to do it."

Alex chuckled.

Health Insurance Premiums: When They Are and Aren't Deductible

Alex asked one of the most common questions: "What about my insurance premiums? They're huge."

Jordan answered carefully.

"When you're self-employed, your health insurance premiums are deductible above the line—meaning you don't have to itemize to claim them. But as a W-2 employee, you can only deduct them as part of medical expenses if they're not paid pre-tax."

Alex sighed. "And mine are pre-tax."

"Then you're already getting a tax break," Jordan explained. "Pre-tax means they're not included in your W-2 wages."

Alex felt a little better. "Good to know."

Example: When the Deduction Kicks In

Jordan offered a practical scenario: "Let's imagine you earn $80,000. Your 7.5 percent threshold is $6,000."

Alex then has:

- $3,500 in dental work
- $1,200 for prescription medications
- $2,800 for specialist visits
- $500 for medical travel expenses
- Total: $8,000.

"You can deduct the amount that exceeds the $6,000 threshold—so $2,000."

Alex nodded. "So it takes a big year of expenses to get any deduction."

"Right," Jordan said, "but when it happens, you'll be glad the deduction exists."

Tax Strategy: Bunching Medical Expenses

Jordan leaned forward. "This deduction lends itself to a powerful planning move: bunching."

Alex looked curious. "You mentioned that with charitable giving."

"Same idea," Jordan said. "Medical expenses are only deductible if they exceed 7.5 percent of AGI. So if you can control the timing of certain procedures, prescriptions, or dental work, you may be able to cluster them into a single year."

"Like getting wisdom teeth removed the same year as a knee surgery?"

"Exactly. If the costs add up in a single year, you may finally cross the threshold."

"And the next year?" Alex asked.

"You keep everything minimal, take the standard deduction, and start fresh."

Alex scribbled notes. "It's like tax judo."

Jordan laughed. "More like tax choreography."

Health Savings Accounts (HSAs): The Triple-Tax Benefit

Alex had heard of HSAs before, but the details were fuzzy.

"Tell me about those," Alex said.

Jordan's eyes lit up. "HSAs are one of the most powerful tools in the tax code."

To qualify, Alex would need to be enrolled in a high-deductible health plan (HDHP). If eligible, the benefits are enormous:

- Contributions are tax-deductible (or pre-tax through payroll).
- Growth is tax-free.
- Withdrawals for qualified medical expenses are tax-free.

"There's nothing else like that," Jordan explained. "Traditional retirement accounts either tax you now or later. HSAs give you a tax break at every step."

Alex asked, "What if I don't spend the money during the year?"

Jordan grinned. "Then it rolls over forever. Many wealthy taxpayers treat HSAs as stealth retirement accounts."

"Really?"

"Oh yes. They contribute every year, invest the funds, and pay medical bills out of pocket—letting the HSA grow until retirement."

Alex shook his head in amazement. "That's... brilliant."

Flexible Spending Accounts (FSAs): A Use-It-or-Lose-It Tool

Jordan explained that FSAs operate differently:

- Contributions are pre-tax.
- Funds generally must be used within the plan year.
- Some employers allow small carryovers or grace periods.

"FSAs are good if you know your expenses ahead of time," Jordan said. "But an HSA gives you much more flexibility."

Alex wrote that down. "HSAs allow rollover; FSAs don't."

"Bingo."

Special Case: Long-Term Care Expenses

Alex's parents were getting older, so the topic hit home.

"Is long-term care deductible?" Alex asked.

Jordan nodded. "Qualified long-term care services are deductible, and premiums for long-term care insurance are deductible up to certain age-based limits."

Jordan added, "It's one of the few ways people can meaningfully offset the crippling costs of elder care."

Alex swallowed hard, thinking of the years ahead.

Two Medical Stories: The Deduction in Action

Jordan shared two contrasting taxpayer examples.

Rebecca—The Poor Taxpayer Mindset

Rebecca had major dental surgery and physical therapy in the same year, totaling $9,000 in expenses. But Rebecca:
- never kept receipts;
- didn't track mileage;
- didn't itemize; and
- never calculated whether she crossed the AGI threshold.

Result: No deduction claimed.

Daniel—The Rich Taxpayer Mindset

Daniel experienced similar medical events, but Daniel:
- saved every invoice;
- tracked mileage to appointments;
- paid certain expenses before year-end to exceed the 7.5 percent threshold; and
- itemized deductions.

Result: Daniel claimed a $3,500 medical expense deduction and significantly reduced federal tax.

Alex sighed. "The difference is organization."

"And awareness," Jordan added. "The tax code rewards the informed."

Chapter Summary

By the end of their discussion, Alex saw medical expenses in a new light. Tax savings may not fix a broken arm or cover therapy bills, but they can soften the financial blow.

Key lessons:

- Medical expenses above 7.5 percent of AGI may be deductible.
- The deduction covers a wide range of necessary treatments and services.
- Proper records are essential.
- HSAs are one of the most powerful tax tools available.
- Strategic timing can turn nondeductible costs into tax savings.
- FSAs and long-term care deductions offer additional avenues for tax relief.

Alex folded the clinic bill and tucked it neatly into a labeled envelope.

"Finally," Alex said, "I understand how to turn my health costs into something that helps me—not just the hospital."

Jordan smiled.

"Now you're thinking like a rich taxpayer."

CHAPTER 7

⋈

Education and Family:
Student Loan Interest, Educator Expenses,
and Other Personal Deductions

One rainy afternoon, Alex sat staring at a familiar number on a loan statement—one that had been followed faithfully since college. The student loan balance wasn't terribly large anymore, but the monthly payments still felt like a stubborn reminder of choices made years ago. Over dinner, Alex vented to Jordan.

"It never ends. I've paid for nearly a decade, and I'm still paying interest. Does any of this ever help me at tax time?"

Jordan smiled knowingly. "It might. If you know the rules."

Alex leaned in. "I'm listening."

The Student Loan Interest Deduction: A Small But Mighty Benefit

Jordan explained that the tax code allows many borrowers to deduct up to $2,500 of student loan interest each year—an above-the-line deduction, meaning Alex does not need to itemize to claim it.

Alex blinked. "So I could have been deducting this for years?"

"Probably," Jordan replied. "Most people qualify at some point, especially early in their careers."

Jordan continued to explain how to qualify:

- The loan must be for qualified higher education expenses.
- The borrower (Alex) must be legally obligated to pay the interest.
- Alex cannot be claimed as a dependent on someone else's tax return.
- The deduction phases out at higher incomes.

Alex frowned. "What phaseout?"

Jordan explained that for 2025, the deduction begins phasing out once income exceeds a certain modified adjusted gross income (MAGI) threshold. Many high-earning professionals lose the deduction as their income rises.

Alex sighed. "So the deduction is strongest when I least have money… and disappears when I start making money?"

Jordan laughed. "Pretty much. But that's exactly when help is needed most."

Example: Alex's Student Loan Deduction

Jordan offered a simple illustration:

- Total interest paid in 2025: $900.
- Alex's income: below the phaseout range.
- Filing status: single.

"You can deduct the full $900," Jordan said. "And since it's above the line, it lowers your adjusted gross income—which can help you qualify for other deductions and credits."

Alex exhaled with relief. "That's the first good news from my student loans in a while."

Education Credits: Powerful, But Not Deductions

Jordan cautioned that student loan interest is not the only education-related tax break—nor the largest.

"Depending on the situation," Jordan said, "taxpayers may claim education credits such as the Lifetime Learning Credit or the American Opportunity Tax Credit."

Alex leaned forward. "So I can double-dip?"

"No," Jordan said firmly. "Credits and deductions can't apply to the same expenses. But education credits reduce tax dollar for dollar, which can be more powerful than a deduction."

Alex wrote a reminder: "Check education credits each year."

Educator Expense Deduction: Relief for Teachers

Alex's sister, Emma, was a middle-school math teacher who often complained about buying classroom supplies with her own money.

"Tell Emma this," Jordan said. "For tax years through 2025, eligible educators can deduct up to $300 of unreimbursed classroom and instructional expenses. For tax year 2026, the limit increases to $350 indexed."

"Always?"

"Yes," Jordan replied. "It's an above-the-line deduction—so it can help whether you itemize or take the standard deduction—as long as the expenses qualify and are unreimbursed."

Then Jordan added something new:

"And beginning in 2026, if she itemizes, she may be able to deduct additional educator expenses on Schedule A, not subject to the usual miscellaneous itemized deduction limits. Just don't double-count the same receipts."

Alex smiled. "She'll be thrilled."

Adoption, Childcare, and Family-Based Deductions

Jordan shifted gears.

"There are other personal deductions people forget—especially families."

Alex pulled out a pen.

1. Adoption Expenses
Adoptive parents may receive tax credits for qualifying adoption expenses. These aren't deductions, but they reduce

tax liability directly and can save thousands.

2. Dependent Care Benefits
Employees who use workplace dependent care accounts can exclude up to a certain amount from income to cover childcare costs.

3. Qualifying Dependent Rules
Alex learned that financially supporting aging parents or relatives might make them dependents for tax purposes, opening the door to additional credits or deductions.

Jordan offered a real-life scenario: "If you pay more than half the support for your elderly mother, she may qualify as your dependent. That can lower your taxable income and expand your filing opportunities."

Alex sat back. "I had no idea."

Jordan nodded. "That's the problem with most taxpayers—they only think about deductions in April, not throughout the year."

Tuition and Fees: A Deduction That Comes and Goes

Alex remembered hearing about a tuition deduction.

"That was the Tuition and Fees Deduction," Jordan explained. "It expired, got renewed, expired again… Congress can't seem to decide what to do with it."

Alex chuckled. "So it's like the boomerang of deductions."

"Exactly."

While it is currently unavailable, Jordan noted that credits and employer-provided educational assistance often fill its place.

Employer-Provided Education Assistance

Jordan emphasized that many employers offer tuition reimbursement programs.

"If your employer pays for your education, up to a certain amount can be excluded from income," Jordan said.

Alex smiled. "So I can further my career and get a tax break?"

Jordan nodded. "That's the spirit."

Two Education Stories: The Rich Taxpayer versus the Poor Taxpayer

Jordan contrasted two employees at the same company.

Case 1: Maya—The Poor Taxpayer Mindset

Maya:

- paid student loan interest;
- lost receipts;
- never checked phaseouts; and
- didn't know about the deduction.

Result: No deduction claimed.

Case 2: Elena—The Rich Taxpayer Mindset

Elena:

- tracked student loan interest.
- claimed the above-the-line deduction.
- used an employer tuition plan to finish a degree; and
- evaluated education credits when taking courses.

Result: Thousands saved over several years.

Alex shook his head. "It really is about awareness."
Jordan nodded. "Knowledge is profit."

Alex Learns a Final Lesson

As Alex gathered the student loan documents that evening, the struggle of years past seemed a little lighter.

Alex realized a few things:

- Borrowing for education is tough—but the tax code offers relief.
- Teachers and educators quietly shoulder expenses, but the IRS acknowledges their burden.
- Family support may unlock additional deductions or

credits.
- Credits, deductions, and employer programs form an ecosystem of savings—if you know where to look.

Jordan summed it up best: "A poor taxpayer treats education as a bill. A rich taxpayer treats it as an opportunity."

CHAPTER 8

ॐ૮ঽ৪

No Tax on Tips:
A New Deduction for Service Workers

Alex had worked plenty of service jobs back in college—waiting tables, running coffee orders, even delivering pizzas on weekends. The memory of hustling for tips was still vivid: long shifts, aching feet, and the unpredictable nature of customer generosity. So when Jordan mentioned a brand-new tax break designed specifically for tip-based workers, Alex's curiosity was instant.

"Wait… a deduction for tips?" Alex asked. "You mean, like… I can deduct the tips I earn?"

Jordan smiled. "Not exactly. But pretty close."

Alex blinked. "Now I'm intrigued."

A Deduction for Tipped Employees—Brand New in 2025

Jordan explained that the One Big Beautiful Bill Act of 2025 introduced a groundbreaking provision: a special deduction—up to $25,000 per year—for individuals earning qualified tips.

Alex raised an eyebrow. "Qualified tips?"

"Yes," Jordan said. "Tips that are legally required to be reported. The same ones employees have always had to tell their employer about."

Jordan continued:

"For years, servers, bartenders, delivery workers, hair stylists, valets—basically anyone who depends on tips—had to treat those tips as fully taxable wages. Now, for the first time, the tax code recognizes the unique burden on tipped workers."

Alex leaned in. "So this deduction reduces taxable income?"

"Exactly," Jordan replied. "Dollar for dollar."

How the No Tax on Tips Deduction Works

Jordan broke it down:

- The deduction is available from 2025 through 2028.
- Eligible taxpayers can deduct up to $25,000 of qualified tips earned and reported to their employer.
- It applies whether you itemize or take the standard deduction.
- You must legally report the tip income (unreported tips do not qualify).
- Tips must come from an occupation where tipping is customary.

Alex laughed. "So no deducting the five bucks Grandma gives you at Thanksgiving?"

"Correct," Jordan said. "The IRS isn't that generous."

Who Qualifies for the Deduction?

Individuals in the following occupations typically qualify:

- Restaurant servers
- Bartenders
- Baristas
- Hotel staff
- Ride-share and delivery drivers
- Casino workers
- Salon and spa professionals
- Valets and parking attendants

Jordan handed Alex a printed IRS notice.

"The IRS will publish and update a list of qualifying occupations each year," Jordan said, "but it's safe to assume that anything traditionally tipped is eligible."

Alex nodded. "Makes sense."

Income Phaseouts: When the Deduction Shrinks

Jordan continued: "There's a catch—not everyone gets the full $25,000 deduction."

Alex sighed. "There's always a catch."

This deduction begins to phase out once a taxpayer's modified adjusted gross income (MAGI) exceeds:

- $150,000 for single filers
- $300,000 for married filing jointly.

Alex tilted his head. "So this is really targeted at working-class and middle-income earners."

"Exactly," Jordan said. "High-income professionals don't qualify—nor should they. This deduction was created for hardworking people who rely on tips to pay their bills."

Example: Maria the Server

Jordan shared a story.

Maria works full-time as a restaurant server, earning:

- $32,000 in wages, and
- $18,000 in reported tips.

Before 2025, Maria would pay income tax on the full $50,000. Now, under the new law:

Maria can deduct up to $18,000 in tips (since it is below the $25,000 cap). That means her taxable income becomes $32,000, not $50,000.

Alex's jaw dropped. "That's massive."

"It is," Jordan agreed. "It's one of the biggest tax breaks service workers have ever received."

Reporting Tips: An IRS Reality Check

Alex remembered the days when tips were scribbled onto napkins for self-tracking—or not tracked at all.

Jordan raised a finger. "Important point: This deduction only applies to tips that are properly reported."

Alex smirked. "So under-the-table tips don't count?"

"Nope," Jordan said. "In fact, if anything, this deduction is a strong incentive to report tips."

From 2025 onward, employers are encouraged—but not required—to report qualified tips separately on W-2 forms. The IRS has provided transition relief for employers in 2025 so they won't be penalized for incorrect reporting during the rollout.

Alex shook his head. "For once, doing the right thing really pays."

Who Should Claim This Deduction?

Jordan explained that the deduction is ideal for:

- younger workers;
- people working service jobs part-time;
- individuals in gig-based, tip-heavy industries;
- people transitioning jobs or earning below six figures; and
- anyone whose taxable income falls squarely in the middle brackets.

"This deduction puts real money back into real pockets," Jordan said. "And because it's above-the-line, it lowers adjusted gross income—which can unlock other deductions and credits."

Alex said, "So it can snowball?"

"Exactly. Everything in the tax world is connected."

Two Tipped Workers: How Mindset Makes the Difference

Jordan described two workers at the same restaurant:

Case 1: Janelle—The Poor Taxpayer Mindset
Janelle:
- reports minimal tips;
- keeps no records;
- doesn't understand the new rule; and
- misses out on the deduction entirely.

Result: Higher taxable income and more tax owed.

Case 2: Priya—The Rich Taxpayer Mindset
Priya:
- keeps accurate tip logs;
- reports tips consistently;
- claims the new deduction; and
- qualifies for additional credits due to lower AGI.

Result: Significant tax savings and financial breathing room.

Alex sighed.
"It all comes back to organization and awareness, doesn't it?"
Jordan nodded. "As always."

Chapter Summary

By the end of their discussion, Alex realized the new tip deduction was transformational for millions of Americans.

Key lessons:

- Tips have historically been fully taxable, but now up to $25,000 per year can be deducted.
- The deduction is available to service workers in tip-intensive occupations.
- It is an above-the-line deduction—available even without itemizing.
- Only reported tips count.
- High earners are phased out.
- Good recordkeeping is essential.

Alex smiled as the conversation wrapped up.

"Back when I waited tables," Alex said, "this would have changed everything."

Jordan nodded. "And now, for a lot of people, it will."

CHAPTER 9

 C3 80

No Tax on Overtime:
Turning Extra Hours into Extra Savings

Alex had been working long hours that month—quarter-end deadlines, late-night project revisions, and even a Saturday shift. When the overtime pay finally hit the paycheck, Alex felt a surge of pride… followed by a familiar frustration.

"It's not fair," Alex said to Jordan. "I work harder, and the IRS takes more. My overtime is taxed like a punishment."

Jordan grinned. "Not anymore."

Alex blinked. "What do you mean?"

"You haven't heard about the No Tax on Overtime deduction, have you?"

Alex stared blankly.

Jordan laughed. "You're going to like this one."

A New Deduction for America's Workforce

The One Big Beautiful Bill Act of 2025 created an unprecedented tax break: a deduction for overtime premium pay—the extra amount paid beyond regular hourly wages.

"Think of it this way," Jordan said. "If you're paid time-and-a-half, the half part is deductible."

Alex raised an eyebrow. "Really?"

"Really," Jordan replied. "And it can add up fast."

The law provides:

- a deduction for qualified overtime pay, meaning the premium portion (the extra half-time) of overtime wages;
- a cap of $12,500 for single filers and $25,000 for married filing jointly;
- eligibility regardless of whether the taxpayer itemizes; and
- applicability from 2025 through 2028.

Alex shook his head in disbelief.
"So Congress is actually rewarding overtime now?"
Jordan nodded. "For once, yes."

What Counts as "Qualified Overtime"?

Jordan explained:
Most hourly workers are entitled to time-and-a-half pay for hours worked beyond forty hours per week under federal and state labor laws. The new tax law allows taxpayers to deduct the premium portion of those wages.

Example:
If Alex earns $20 per hour:
- Regular wage = $20
- Overtime wage = $30
- Premium portion = $10

That $10 premium portion is considered qualified overtime compensation and counts toward the deduction.

Alex asked, "So only the extra part is deductible?"
"Correct," Jordan said. "You still pay tax on your base wage—but not on the overtime bonus portion."

Who Qualifies?

Jordan listed the eligible categories:

- Non-exempt hourly workers.
- Employees with employer-reported overtime wages.
- Workers in industries such as manufacturing, retail, hospitality, transportation, and healthcare.
- Exempt salaried employees receiving fixed salaries do not qualify unless their employer separately compensates overtime at a premium rate.

"This deduction was created for people who actually clock overtime hours," Jordan said.

Alex nodded. "Makes sense."

Income Phaseouts: When the Deduction Shrinks

Like the tip deduction, the overtime deduction phases out at higher incomes:

- $150,000 MAGI for single filers
- $300,000 MAGI for married filers.

Jordan explained: "This isn't intended for high-income people. It's designed for the workforce that actually depends on overtime to live."

Alex laughed. "So it's not for executives pulling sixty-hour weeks."

"Exactly."

Example: Alex's Overtime Deduction

Jordan ran through a real-life scenario.

Suppose Alex earns:

- Base pay: $52,000
- Overtime premium (extra half-time wages): $6,400

"If you're below the income threshold," Jordan said, "you can deduct the entire $6,400 from taxable income."

Alex's eyes widened. "That's a huge savings."

"Yup. And because it's above the line, it reduces your AGI, which can increase your eligibility for other deductions and credits."

A New Incentive to Report Overtime Accurately

Jordan emphasized the importance of payroll reporting:

"Your employer will report qualified overtime on your W-2. But even if they don't separate the numbers perfectly in 2025, the IRS has announced transition relief—no penalties while employers update their systems."

Alex asked, "So if the employer messes up the reporting, I'm not punished for it?"

Jordan nodded. "Correct. But you still need to keep your pay stubs."

Alex agreed. "Fair enough."

Overtime for Side Jobs and Multiple Employers

Alex often picked up weekend shifts for another company during peak months.

Jordan explained: "Good news—if you work overtime for multiple employers, the deduction applies per taxpayer, not per job."

"So the cap is $12,500 for me total, even if it comes from two places?"

"Exactly."

Alex grinned. "That's going to help a lot of people."

Two Overtime Workers: Why Mindset Matters

Jordan described two workers at the same warehouse.

Case 1: Kevin—The Poor Taxpayer Mindset
Kevin:
- works overtime frequently;
- doesn't track hours;

- doesn't review his W-2; and
- has no idea the deduction exists.

Result: Kevin claims zero of the deduction and pays tax on all overtime.

Case 2: Deja—The Rich Taxpayer Mindset

Deja:

- verifies overtime premium amounts;
- saves pay stubs;
- understands the new deduction; and
- claims $7,800 of qualified overtime.

Result: Deja reduces taxable income dramatically and qualifies for additional tax credits due to a lower AGI.

Alex sighed. "Poor Kevin. That was me for years."
Jordan chuckled. "And now you're Deja."

Chapter Summary

Alex leaned back in the chair, imagining the possibilities. For millions of Americans, overtime had always been a bittersweet blessing—more money earned but more taxes withheld. Now, the tax code finally acknowledged the effort.

Key lessons:

- The overtime premium portion (time-and-a-half "extra") is deductible.
- The deduction is worth up to $12,500 single, $25,000 married.
- It applies for tax years 2025 through 2028.
- It is an above-the-line deduction.
- Only workers receiving true overtime pay qualify.
- High earners are phased out.
- Proper reporting and recordkeeping are essential.

Alex looked at Jordan and said:
"You know… I don't mind working hard. But it feels a lot

better when the IRS doesn't take a bite out of my extra shifts."

Jordan nodded. "That's the idea. Work hard—and keep more of what you earn."

CHAPTER 10

C3ED

No Tax on Wheels:
The Car Loan Interest Deduction

Alex had just bought a new car. It wasn't flashy—just a reliable mid-sized sedan with good mileage and enough room for weekend trips. When the first car payment hit, Alex winced at the amount of interest built into the loan. It wasn't painful… but it wasn't pleasant, either.

Over coffee, Alex shared the news with Jordan.

"New car, new loan. I guess interest is just part of the deal."

Jordan smiled. "Sure is. But did you know 2025 changed everything about car loan interest?"

Alex looked confused. "What do you mean?"

Jordan leaned closer.

"There's a brand-new deduction that applies to personal car loan interest. And almost no one knows it exists yet."

A First-in-History Deduction for Personal Car Loan Interest

For decades, taxpayers were allowed to deduct interest on mortgages, student loans, and certain business loans.

But never on personal car loans.

"That changed with the One Big Beautiful Bill Act of 2025," Jordan said. "Congress introduced something they called 'No Tax on Car Loan Interest.'"

Alex blinked. "So I can deduct the interest on my car loan…

even though it's for personal use?"

"Exactly," Jordan replied. "For the first time ever."

This deduction is available for tax years 2025 through 2028, and it applies only to interest paid on qualifying new vehicles purchased and financed during that time.

Alex sat up straighter.

"That could save me a fortune."

What Vehicles Qualify?

Jordan outlined the rules.

To claim the deduction, the taxpayer must have:

- purchased a new vehicle—not used, not leased;
- purchased a passenger automobile, SUV, truck, or motorcycle;
- purchased a vehicle with final assembly in the United States; and
- taken out a loan (cash purchases don't qualify because there's no interest to deduct).

"So my sedan qualifies?" Alex asked.

"Check your window sticker," Jordan said. "It lists the final assembly point. If it's US-assembled, you're good."

Alex made a mental note to review the sticker tucked in the glove compartment.

How Much Interest Is Deductible?

The deduction is capped:

- $10,000 of interest per year for single filers.
- $20,000 for married couples filing jointly.

Alex's eyes widened. "I don't think I'll hit those limits."

Jordan laughed. "Most people won't. But the cap is generous."

Income Phaseouts: Not Everyone Gets the Full Deduction

Like the new tip and overtime deductions, the car loan interest deduction phases out.

Jordan explained:

- Full deduction is available up to $100,000 MAGI for single filers.
- Full deduction is available up to $200,000 MAGI for married filing jointly.
- The deduction fully phases out at much higher incomes.

"So it's meant for the middle class," Alex said.

"Exactly."

Example: Alex's New Car Loan

Jordan pulled out a notebook.

Suppose Alex's loan has:

- Loan amount: $24,000
- Interest rate: 6 percent
- First-year interest: $1,300

"You can deduct the entire $1,300," Jordan said. "It's an above-the-line deduction."

Alex's jaw dropped. "Above the line? Even if I don't itemize?"

"Correct. This deduction reduces your AGI directly."

Alex smiled. "That's huge."

What About Used Cars?

Alex asked the next obvious question.

"Can I deduct interest on a used car?"

"Unfortunately, no," Jordan said. "Congress limited the deduction to new vehicles only, partly to boost domestic manufacturing."

Alex frowned. "So no help for used-car buyers."
Jordan nodded. "Not with this deduction."

What About Business Vehicles?

This time Jordan shook his head.

"The new deduction applies only to personal-use vehicles. If a vehicle is used more than 50 percent for business, you already have access to business deductions under Section 162 or depreciation rules."

Alex laughed. "So this is basically the 'everyday driver' deduction?"

"Exactly."

Can You Deduct Interest on More Than One Car?

Jordan answered: "Yes—but only up to the annual limit. So if you and a spouse each buy a qualifying car, and you file jointly, you could deduct up to $20,000 in interest combined."

Alex grinned.

"That's... shockingly generous."

Jordan nodded. "One of the biggest middle-class tax perks in decades."

Recordkeeping Requirements

Jordan explained that taxpayers need:

- a copy of the retail installment contract (car loan agreement);
- year-end loan statements showing interest paid; and
- proof that the car was purchased new and has US final assembly.

Alex sighed in relief. "That's easy. My lender already sends the statement."

"That's exactly why Congress structured it this way," Jordan said. "Simple compliance."

Two Drivers: A Tale of Missed and Captured Opportunity

Jordan gave an example of two individuals.

Case 1: Brian—The Poor Taxpayer Mindset

Brian buys a new US-assembled car but:

- doesn't read the tax rules,
- doesn't track interest, and
- doesn't claim the deduction.

Result: Brian pays hundreds more in tax unnecessarily.

Case 2: Lila—The Rich Taxpayer Mindset

Lila:

- checks the assembly point,
- saves all loan documents,
- claims the car loan interest deduction, and
- reduces AGI, improving eligibility for other deductions.

Result: Lila significantly lowers her tax liability.

Alex chuckled. "Let me guess—I used to be Brian."
Jordan nodded. "Not anymore."

Chapter Summary

Alex now realized that even everyday purchases—like a car—can create tax benefits if approached strategically.

Key lessons:

- The No Tax on Car Loan Interest deduction is brand new (2025 through 2028).
- It covers interest on new, US-assembled, personally used vehicles.
- The cap is $10,000 single, $20,000 married.
- It is an above-the-line deduction.
- It phases out for higher incomes.
- Used cars and leases do not qualify.

Alex leaned back and smiled.

"For the first time," Alex said, "my car payment doesn't feel so… painful."

Jordan nodded.

"That's the power of tax knowledge. You start seeing savings everywhere."

CHAPTER 11

CB&O

Deductions for the Side Hustle: Ordinary and Necessary Business Expenses

lex had always admired people who ran side businesses. Freelance designers, weekend photographers, Uber drivers, tutors—they all seemed to have some extra spark, a little more control over their income. So when Alex finally began earning money from a weekend consulting gig, it felt like a small victory.

That feeling didn't last long.

When tax season rolled around, Alex stared at the 1099 form from the client with a sense of dread.

"Why does it say I made so much?" Alex groaned to Jordan. "I didn't keep that much."

Jordan smiled knowingly. "Because you haven't learned the secret of the side hustle yet."

Alex looked confused. "Secret?"

Jordan nodded. "The tax code treats business owners completely differently than employees. You get deductions that regular W-2 earners can only dream of."

Alex leaned forward. "Teach me."

The Magical World of Business Deductions

Jordan explained that once you have self-employment income, even from a small side business, you immediately gain access to a powerful set of tax deductions that exist under Internal Revenue Code §162.

"These are called ordinary and necessary business expenses," Jordan said. "Meaning expenses that are common, accepted, and helpful for your line of work."

Alex raised an eyebrow.

"So… what counts?"

"More than you think," Jordan replied.

What Makes an Expense Deductible?

Jordan spelled out the two-part test used by the IRS:

- The expense must be ordinary—typical in your industry.
- The expense must be necessary—helpful or appropriate for running the business.

Alex scribbled notes. "Ordinary *and* necessary. Got it."

Jordan continued: "For your consulting business, things like software, office supplies, equipment, online subscriptions, and travel to client meetings all qualify."

Alex's eyes widened.

"I spend money on all of that."

Jordan grinned.

"And now it all becomes deductible."

Example: Alex's First Side Hustle Year

Let's say Alex earns $8,000 from consulting work in 2025. Alex also spent:

- $600 on software
- $450 on office supplies
- $300 on advertising
- $150 on professional courses
- $120 on cloud storage

- $75 on business cards
- Total expenses: $1,695

"If you don't claim these deductions," Jordan said, "you pay tax on the full $8,000. But if you deduct the $1,695, your taxable business income drops to $6,305."

Alex smiled. "That feels fair."

"It's more than fair," Jordan said. "It's how wealth begins."

Common Deductions for Side Hustles

Jordan created a list of typical deductions:

1. Office Supplies and Equipment
Pens, paper, external monitors, printers, hard drives—anything used in the business.

2. Software and Online Tools
Subscriptions for project management, design apps, accounting tools, backup services, and cloud drives count toward the deductible.

3. Advertising and Marketing
Website costs, social media ads, business cards.

4. Business Meals (with a Client or Partner)
Fifty percent deductible when used for business discussions.

5. Education and Training
Courses, webinars, certifications related to the business.

6. Professional Services
Fees paid to accountants, attorneys, or consultants.

7. Communications Costs
Part of your phone bill or internet bill may be deductible if

used for business.

"But be careful," Jordan said. "You can only deduct the business portion—not your entire Netflix subscription."

Alex laughed. "Good to know."

The Power of Keeping Good Records

Jordan emphasized a lesson repeated in nearly every chapter:

"The IRS doesn't require perfection. They require proof."

Alex asked, "Like receipts?"

"Yes," Jordan said. "Receipts, invoices, bank statements, mileage logs—everything."

Jordan continued: "Think of recordkeeping as the gatekeeper. A rich taxpayer tracks expenses in real time. A poor taxpayer reconstructs them in April… or guesses."

Alex sighed. "Sounds like I used to be a poor taxpayer."

"Not anymore," Jordan said.

The Smartphone Rule

Jordan pointed to Alex's phone.

"You use that thing for work sometimes, right?"

"Of course."

"Then part of it is deductible."

Alex blinked. "Really?"

"Absolutely," Jordan said. "If 30 percent of your usage is business—email, calls, apps—you deduct 30 percent of the phone bill."

Alex looked sheepish.

"I never thought of that."

Jordan chuckled.

"The tax code rewards people who think like business owners."

Transportation Expenses: A Preview of Chapter 13

If Alex drives to meet clients, shop for supplies, or travel for business, mileage is deductible. Jordan hinted that a full chapter on travel and vehicles was coming soon.

"For now," Jordan said, "just remember: your commute to a

regular job is not deductible. But driving for your side business usually is."

Alex made a note.

"Business miles good. Commute bad."

What About Meals and Clothing?

Alex asked the classic question: "Can I deduct clothes for my business?"

Jordan shook his head. "Only if they're uniforms or clothing unsuitable for everyday wear. A suit for a consulting meeting? Not deductible."

"And meals?"

"Meals are deductible only when they have a business purpose—meeting with a client, partner, or prospect. No deduction for grabbing lunch alone."

Alex nodded slowly.

"Okay… makes sense."

Self-Employment Tax: The Part Everyone Forgets

Jordan leaned in with a serious tone.

"When you earn side income, you're considered both the employee and the employer for Social Security and Medicare taxes."

Alex winced. "That sounds expensive."

"It is," Jordan admitted. "But you get to deduct half of your self-employment tax as an above-the-line deduction."

"So the IRS gives with one hand and takes with the other?"

Jordan grinned. "Welcome to entrepreneurship."

Two Freelancers: A Tale of Mindset

Jordan illustrated with an example:

Case 1: Leo—The Poor Taxpayer Mindset
Leo earns $5,000 from freelance photography but:
- keeps no receipts;
- doesn't track mileage;

- doesn't understand deductions; and
- reports the full $5,000 as taxable income.

Result: Leo pays tax on all $5,000, plus full self-employment tax.

Case 2: Serena—The Rich Taxpayer Mindset

Serena earns the same $5,000 but:

- tracks expenses;
- deduces $1,400 of equipment and software;
- deduces business mileage;
- claims half her self-employment tax; and
- lowers her taxable income dramatically.

Result: Serena keeps far more money than Leo.

Alex shook his head. "Same income, different results."
Jordan nodded. "That difference is mindset."

Chapter Summary

Alex now understood that even a small side hustle can create powerful tax-saving opportunities.

Key lessons:

- Business owners can deduct ordinary and necessary expenses.
- Software, supplies, advertising, education, and part of phone or internet can be deductible.
- Good recordkeeping is essential.
- Self-employment tax is higher—but partially deductible.
- The difference between owing tax and saving money is all about awareness and intentionality.

Alex finally smiled. "I always thought a side hustle was just more work. Now I see it's also more opportunity."
Jordan nodded. "Exactly. A side hustle is the gateway to the tax world the wealthy have used for decades."

CHAPTER 12

ℭℨℬ

Home Office, Big Savings:
Turning Your Living Space into a Deduction

A lex stared at the spare bedroom with mixed emotions. It had always been a catch-all space—part guest room, part storage area, part "I'll organize this later." But now that Alex's side consulting work was growing, the room suddenly looked… purposeful.

Jordan stopped by one evening and saw the transformation beginning.

"Looks like you're setting up a home office," Jordan said with approval.

Alex nodded. "I figured I should finally have a proper workspace."

Jordan grinned. "Congrats—you've just opened the door to one of the most misunderstood and underused tax deductions in America."

Alex laughed. "You mean this room can save me money?"

Jordan walked inside and ran a hand along the desk. "If you use it correctly, absolutely."

The Home Office Deduction: A Powerful Yet Misunderstood Tool

Jordan sat down and explained the basics.

"The home office deduction allows self-employed individuals

to deduct expenses for the part of their home used regularly and exclusively for business."

Alex tilted his head. "What does 'exclusively' mean?"

"It means this space must be used only for business—not personal activities. Not a guest room, not a workout corner, not your gaming lounge. Just business."

Alex sighed. "So I can't keep the treadmill in here?"

Jordan smirked. "Not if you want the deduction."

What Qualifies as a Home Office?

Jordan outlined two requirements:

- Exclusive use: A clearly defined area used only for business. It doesn't have to be a full room—it can be part of one—but it must be exclusive.
- Regular use: Meaning it is used consistently, not occasionally.

Alex nodded. "Okay, that's doable."

Then Jordan added the most important qualification:

- Principal place of business: Your home office must be your primary location for administrative or management activities—unless you meet clients there, in which case the rule is even more flexible.

Alex raised a brow. "So even if I visit clients occasionally, I can still qualify?"

"Yes," Jordan said. "If your administrative work—emails, billing, planning—occurs here, it counts."

Two Deduction Methods: Simplified versus Actual Expenses

Jordan explained that the IRS offers two ways to claim the deduction.

1. Simplified Method
A flat rate per square foot of office space—easy, clean, and limited.
- $5 per square foot
- Maximum of 300 square feet
- Maximum annual deduction: $1,500

Alex smiled. "That sounds easy."
"It is," Jordan said. "But for many people, the actual expense method is far more valuable."

2. Actual Expense Method
This method allows you to deduct a percentage of real home expenses:
- Rent or mortgage interest
- Property taxes
- Utilities
- Homeowners insurance
- Repairs and maintenance
- Depreciation (if you own the home)

The deduction is based on the proportion of your home used for business. For example, if Alex's office is 10 percent of the home, then 10 percent of these eligible expenses are deductible.

Alex's eyes widened. "So part of my rent becomes deductible?"
"Exactly," Jordan said. "And part of your utilities too."

Example: Alex's Home Office Calculation
Jordan walked Alex through a practical example:

- Home size: 1,200 square feet
- Office size: 120 square feet
- Percentage: 10 percent
- Annual rent: $18,000
- Utilities: $2,400

- Insurance: $600
- Repairs: $300
- Total expenses = $21,300
- 10 percent of $21,300 = $2,130 deduction

Alex's jaw dropped.

"That's... way more than the $1,500 simplified method."

Jordan nodded.

"Exactly why many people choose the actual method."

Repairs versus Improvements: Know the Difference

Alex asked whether a recent paint job counted as a deductible repair.

Jordan explained:

- Direct repairs to the office (painting, fixing light fixtures) are fully deductible.
- Indirect repairs (fixing a furnace that heats the whole home) are deducted by percentage.
- Improvements (adding a deck, renovating a kitchen) must be depreciated, not deducted all at once—unless they specifically benefit the office.

Alex looked puzzled. "So painting the office is deductible, but painting my living room isn't?"

Jordan smiled. "That's right. Think like a business owner."

The Exclusive Use Rule: Where Most People Slip Up

Jordan warned Alex not to treat the rule lightly.

"If the IRS audits your return and finds your office doubles as a guest bedroom, the deduction gets denied."

Alex said, "So no bed, no yoga mat, no TV?"

Jordan nodded. "Correct."

"But I can keep office supplies here, right?"

"Of course. Anything used for the business is fine."

Home Office for Employees? No Longer Deductible

Alex asked a question that many people forget: "What if I start working from home for my employer? Can I deduct this office then?"

Jordan shook his head. "For W-2 employees, the home office deduction was eliminated in 2018 and remains unavailable under the 2025 tax rules."

Alex frowned. "Even if my employer doesn't reimburse me?"

"Still no," Jordan confirmed. "But if you're self-employed—even part time—you're eligible."

Alex smiled again. "So this office helps my side business, not my day job."

"Exactly."

The Depreciation Catch for Homeowners

Jordan raised one more important point.

"If you own your home and use the actual expense method, you must depreciate the office portion of the home each year."

Alex asked, "Is that bad?"

"Not at all," Jordan said. "Depreciation increases your deduction now. The catch is when you sell the home."

Jordan continued:

- You must recapture (repay tax on) the depreciation taken.
- But only the depreciation—not the home's general appreciation—gets taxed.
- The rest of your home may still qualify for the tax-free Section 121 exclusion ($250,000 single, $500,000 married).

Alex nodded. "So it's a tradeoff."

Jordan smiled. "A smart one if you track it properly."

Two Home Workers: A Tale of Missteps and Mastery

Case 1: Tara—The Poor Taxpayer Mindset
Tara uses her dining table for work, spreads papers everywhere, and calls it a "home office." She:
- fails the exclusive-use test,
- has no dedicated space, but
- claims the deduction anyway.

Result: Deduction denied during audit, causing stress, penalties, and frustration.

Case 2: Omar—The Rich Taxpayer Mindset
Omar:
- dedicates a spare room,
- keeps it exclusively for his online tutoring business,
- tracks expenses carefully, and
- claims the deduction correctly.

Result: Significant annual tax savings and clean compliance.

Alex sighed. "I see the difference."

Jordan nodded. "Home office deductions reward structure. And punish sloppiness."

Chapter Summary

By the end of the discussion, Alex saw the spare bedroom in a radically different light.

Key lessons:

- Self-employed taxpayers can deduct part of their home expenses through the home office deduction.
- The space must be used regularly and exclusively for business.
- You can choose between the simplified method and actual expenses.
- Actual expenses often yield far larger deductions.
- Recordkeeping is essential.

- Homeowners must depreciate the business portion.
- W-2 employees cannot claim a home office deduction.

Alex looked around the freshly organized office with pride. "For the first time," he said, "this room feels like it's earning its keep."

Jordan smiled. "That's because it finally is."

CHAPTER 13

ᘏᘖ

On the Road:
Travel, Meals, and Vehicle Deductions

Alex had always liked the feeling of motion—the quiet hum of the road, the sense that every stop had a purpose. But once the business started, every mile came with a new question: Is this deductible?

One afternoon, Alex dropped a stack of receipts and a half-filled mileage log on Jordan's desk.

"I know the rule is 'business only,'" Alex said, "but the lines get blurry. And I keep hearing that 2026 changed something about meals. Can you give me the real road map?"

Jordan nodded. "Sure. The IRS doesn't reward driving or eating. It rewards business purpose, documentation, and the right method. Let's build your map one lane at a time."

Business Mileage: Turning Every Business Drive into a Deduction

Jordan started with the simplest choice: You can deduct vehicle use two different ways—the IRS standard mileage rate, or your actual vehicle expenses. You do not get to double dip for the same mile.

"If you want simple," Jordan said, "standard mileage is usually the cleanest. Track business miles, multiply by the year's IRS mileage rate, and add tolls and parking."

"And actual expenses?" Alex asked.

"That means gas, insurance, repairs, registration, and depreciation—multiplied by your business-use percentage. More paperwork, but sometimes bigger."

Jordan tapped the mileage log.

"Either way, the rule is the same: If you can't prove the business miles, the deduction is just a story."

- Key reminder: Commuting (home to your main work location and back) is personal and not deductible. Business mileage is travel between business stops—client visits, supply runs, jobsites, meetings, and trips between locations.

Travel versus Commuting: The Overnight Rule

Next, Jordan drew a line between local driving and travel.

"Travel expenses are for trips away from your tax home that are long enough to require sleep or rest," Jordan said. "Transportation, lodging, and other ordinary and necessary business travel costs can be deductible."

Alex nodded. "So a one-day conference across town isn't travel. A two-day conference out of state usually is."

"Exactly. Keep the agenda, keep the receipts, and write down the business purpose. If you mix business and personal days, you need to allocate."

Meals: The 50 Percent Rule (and the 2026 Shift for Some Employer Meals)

"Now meals," Jordan said, "are where people get sloppy."

Most business meals are only 50 percent deductible. The meal has to be an ordinary and necessary business expense, not lavish or extravagant, and the taxpayer (or an employee) generally needs to be present. Document who you met, where, when, and what business was discussed.

Entertainment is different. Tickets, golf, sporting events, and similar entertainment are generally not deductible—even if business is discussed. If food is purchased separately (and separately stated) from entertainment, the food may still qualify for the 50 percent meal deduction.

Then Jordan added the 2026 update: "Beginning in 2026, employers generally cannot deduct the cost of food and beverages they provide to employees as de minimis fringe meals or for the convenience of the employer—think office snacks, an on-site cafeteria, or routine working lunches—unless a specific statutory exception applies. The meals can still be excluded from the employee's income in many cases, but the employer deduction is much narrower than it used to be."

"So if I buy lunch for the team in the office, I might not get a deduction anymore?" Alex asked.

"Right, not in the usual way. There are exceptions, and one common workaround is treating meals as taxable compensation when appropriate, but you should plan it deliberately instead of guessing."

Vehicle Write-Offs: When the Car Becomes an Asset

"What about writing off the car itself?" Alex asked.

"That's where depreciation and expensing rules come in," Jordan said. "If you use the actual-expense method, you may be able to depreciate the business portion of the vehicle—but there are special limits for many passenger vehicles, and you have to track business use carefully."

Jordan pointed to the next chapter. "We'll cover depreciation, Section 179, and bonus depreciation there. For now, remember: the IRS loves mileage logs and hates estimates."

Road-Test Checklist: Stay Audit-Ready

Before Alex left, Jordan offered a simple checklist:

1) Pick a method (standard mileage or actual) and keep records that match the method.

2) Log business miles contemporaneously—date, destination, business purpose, and miles.

3) Separate meals from entertainment on receipts. If food

is part of an entertainment event, make sure it is separately stated.

4) For travel, keep proof of business purpose (agenda, emails, meeting notes) and allocate when there is a personal component.

Alex tucked the notebook under an arm. "So the road map is simple: business purpose, clean records, and no fairy tales."

Jordan smiled. "Exactly. The IRS doesn't mind deductions. It minds imagination."

CHAPTER 14

CЗᏰᎧ

Tools of the Trade:
Depreciation and Section 179 Expensing

Alex stood in an electronics aisle staring at a laptop that looked like it could run a small spaceship.

"Two thousand dollars," Alex muttered. "That's a painful click."

Jordan grinned. "Only if you buy it like a consumer. If you buy it like an owner, the tax code helps you share the pain."

Depreciation: Spreading the Deduction Over Time

Depreciation is the default rule for most business assets that last more than one year. Instead of deducting the full cost at once, you generally recover the cost over the asset's useful life using IRS depreciation schedules.

"The IRS is basically saying: if the tool helps you earn money for several years, the write-off usually happens over several years too," Jordan explained.

Two concepts matter more than almost anything else: 1) the asset has to be placed in service (ready and available for business use) by year-end; and 2) you can only deduct the business-use percentage.

Section 179: The Upfront Write-Off Button

Section 179 is an election that can let you expense qualifying business property immediately rather than depreciating it over time.

For tax years beginning in 2026, the maximum Section 179 deduction is $2,560,000. The deduction begins to phase out once total qualifying property placed in service exceeds $4,090,000.

There is also a special limit for certain sport utility vehicles—for 2026, the maximum Section 179 deduction for qualifying SUVs is $32,000.

"Here's the catch," Jordan said. "Section 179 generally cannot create a loss by itself. If the business doesn't have enough taxable income, the unused amount carries forward."

Bonus Depreciation: Back to 100 Percent

Then Jordan delivered the headline that changed the math for many owners: "One hundred percent bonus depreciation is back and made permanent. For qualified property acquired and placed in service after January 19, 2025, you can generally deduct 100 percent of the cost in the first year."

Unlike Section 179, bonus depreciation can generally create or increase a net operating loss, which can matter in high-investment years.

179 versus Bonus: Choosing the Right Tool

"So which one do I use?" Alex asked.

"Think of Section 179 as selective and controllable," Jordan said. "You can pick which assets to expense and how much. Bonus depreciation is broader and more automatic unless you elect out."

Planning often comes down to your income level, how stable your profits are, and whether you want deductions now or later.

Example: Alex Buys the Laptop
Alex bought the $2,000 laptop and put it to work immediately.

"If it's used more than 50 percent for business," Jordan said, "you can usually choose to expense it (Section 179), claim 100 percent bonus depreciation (if eligible), or depreciate it over time. The best answer depends on what the rest of your tax year looks like."

Common Traps That Turn Write-Offs into Headaches

Jordan ended with warnings Alex could not ignore:

- Buying an asset but not placing it in service by year-end.
- Claiming 100 percent business use without proof.
- Mixing personal and business purchases without tracking the business percentage.

Alex sighed. "So the purchase isn't the hard part. The proof is."

"Exactly," Jordan said. "Buy smart. Document smarter."

CHAPTER 15

०३৪৩

The 20 Percent Bonus:
The Qualified Business Income
(QBI) Deduction

By the time Alex reached chapter 15, something had changed.

Expenses no longer felt like random receipts. They felt like levers.

"So tell me about this 20 percent thing," Alex said one evening, pointing at a note that read: "QBI = magic?"

Jordan laughed. "Not magic. A deduction. But yes, it can feel like one."

QBI in Plain English

The qualified business income deduction (often called the Section 199A deduction) can allow many owners of sole proprietorships, partnerships, and S corporations to deduct up to 20 percent of qualified business income. It can also apply to 20 percent of qualified REIT dividends and qualified publicly traded partnership income.

"QBI is basically your net business profit," Jordan said, "with some important exclusions—like reasonable compensation paid to an S corporation owner, most investment income, and capital gains."

OBBBA Made the Deduction Permanent—and Expanded the Phase-In Range

Under the One Big Beautiful Bill Act, the QBI deduction no longer sunsets after 2025. It is now permanent.

For 2026, the income threshold where wage-and-property limits and specified-service limits begin is $201,750 for most single filers (and other non-joint filers) and $403,500 for married filing jointly.

The limits phase in over a larger range than before. For 2026, the phase-in ends at $276,750 for most non-joint filers and $553,500 for married filing jointly (a $75,000 and $150,000 phase-in range, respectively).

"Translation," Jordan said. "More people in the middle-high income zone can still get at least a partial deduction, instead of falling off a cliff."

W-2 Wages and Property: Why the IRS Cares

Once you're in the phase-in zone (and above it), the QBI deduction can be limited based on W-2 wages paid by the business and the cost of certain depreciable property (often called UBIA).

"It encourages businesses to pay wages and invest in assets," Jordan explained. "Which is exactly why entity choice, payroll strategy, and depreciation planning all start to overlap."

Specified Service Trades or Businesses

Some businesses—especially certain professional service fields— face additional limits as income rises. In that phase-in range, the deduction can shrink, and above the range it can disappear for a specified service trade or business.

"The detail matters," Jordan warned. "Two businesses that look similar can be treated differently depending on how the income is earned."

New Minimum QBI Deduction for Active Owners

Beginning in 2026, there is a new minimum QBI deduction

designed for small, active businesses.

If your total QBI from one or more active qualified trades or businesses is at least $1,000, and you materially participate in the business, you are eligible for a minimum QBI deduction of $400 (or your regular calculated deduction, if higher). The $1,000 threshold and $400 minimum are indexed for inflation after 2026.

"It's a floor," Jordan said. "It makes sure that an active small business gets at least some benefit, even if the 20 percent math would be smaller."

Example: Alex's Side Business

Alex pulled up the books. "If my side business nets $20,000, the headline deduction is about $4,000, right?"

"Often, yes," Jordan said. "But the exact deduction can be limited by taxable income and, at higher income levels, wage and property limits. This is why you run the numbers instead of guessing."

Alex scribbled in the margin: "Plan wages. Track profit. Run the QBI test before December."

CHAPTER 16

ᥴ੪ᏱᏕᎧ

Super-Sized Savings:
Advanced Retirement and
Deferred Compensation Strategies

lex had always treated retirement as a distant future problem. Then the business started producing real income—and real tax bills.

Over lunch, Jordan slid a notepad across the table.

"Welcome to the big leagues," Jordan said. "This is where the wealthy stop thinking in April and start planning in January."

The 2026 Contribution Limits: Know the Guardrails

Jordan wrote three numbers in bold: contribute, defer, compound.

For 2026, the elective deferral limit for 401(k), 403(b), most 457 plans, and the federal thrift savings plan (TSP) is $24,500.

If you are age fifty or older, the standard catch-up contribution limit is $8,000 in 2026.

If you are age sixty, sixty-one, sixty-two, or sixty-three, a higher catch-up limit applies in 2026: $11,250.

IRAs also increased in 2026: the Individual Retirement Arrangement (IRA) contribution limit is $7,500, with a catch-up contribution of $1,100 for age fifty and older.

"The limits change," Jordan said, "but the principle doesn't: tax-advantaged accounts are legal time machines."

SEP IRA versus Solo 401(k): Two Lanes, Different Speed Limits

For self-employed owners, the vehicle matters.

A Simplified Employee Pension (SEP) IRA is often easy to set up and fund, but the contribution formula is employer-based. A solo 401(k) can allow an owner to contribute both as employee and employer, which can increase flexibility—especially when income is high.

"Pick the plan that matches how you earn," Jordan said. "And pick it early enough to actually use it."

Cash Balance and Defined Benefit Plans: When You Need a Bigger Bucket

Jordan leaned in. "If your income is high and consistent, a cash balance plan can allow very large contributions—sometimes far beyond what a 401(k) alone allows."

"Sounds perfect," Alex said.

"It can be," Jordan replied, "but it comes with real obligations: required funding, actuarial calculations, and long-term commitment. It's a strategy, not a shortcut."

Deferred Compensation: Paying Yourself Later on Purpose

For executives and some business owners, nonqualified deferred compensation can shift income into future years. The rules are strict (including Section 409A timing rules), and mistakes can be expensive.

"Deferral only works if it is documented before the money is earned," Jordan warned. "No retroactive decisions."

Roth versus Pre-Tax: The Tax Rate Chess Match

Alex asked the question everyone asks: "Roth or traditional?"

"It's not religion," Jordan said. "It's tax rate management. If you expect higher tax rates later, Roth can be powerful. If you're in a peak-earning year, pre-tax deferrals can reduce the current hit. The best answer is often a blend."

Alex left lunch with one clear rule: wealthy people do not wait for tax season to decide where their income should land.

93

CHAPTER 17

03⁓80

Real Estate Riches:
Advanced Property Tax Strategies for High Earners

At an open house, Alex watched people walk through a property like they were shopping for paint colors. Jordan walked through like he was shopping for deductions.

"Real estate is one of the few places where the tax code lets you deduct a cost even as the asset can grow in value," Jordan said.

Depreciation: The Paper Loss That Can Create Real Savings

Rental real estate is generally depreciated over long schedules (for example, residential rental buildings over 27.5 years and many commercial buildings over thirty-nine years).

"Depreciation is a non-cash expense," Jordan said. "But the tax savings are real cash."

Cost Segregation + 100 percent Bonus Depreciation

A cost segregation study can reclassify parts of a building into shorter-lived components (like certain land improvements, specialty electrical, or personal property).

With 100 percent bonus depreciation made permanent for

qualified property acquired and placed in service after January 19, 2025, many of those shorter-lived components may be eligible for immediate expensing.

"This is powerful," Jordan warned, "which is why you document it properly. Cost seg is not a vibe. It's engineering and tax law."

Short-Term Rentals and the Passive Loss Puzzle

Real estate losses are often limited by the passive activity rules. But short-term rentals can behave differently if the average rental period is short and the owner materially participates.

"If it's structured and operated the right way," Jordan said, "a short-term rental can sometimes generate deductions that are easier to use. But the facts matter: average stay length, services provided, and your participation."

Real Estate Professional Status: The High Bar

For larger portfolios, some taxpayers try to qualify as a real estate professional to treat rental real estate losses as non-passive.

Jordan summarized the core idea: "It generally requires substantial time in real property trades or businesses—and the documentation to prove it."

Excess Business Loss Limitation: The Yearly Speed Bump

Even when losses are allowed, another rule can limit how much business loss you can use in one year.

For taxable years beginning in 2026, the excess business loss threshold is $256,000 ($512,000 for joint returns). Losses above that threshold are generally carried forward as part of a net operating loss.

1031 Exchanges: Still a Core Real Estate Tool

A like-kind exchange under Section 1031 can defer gain when exchanging real property used in a trade or business or held for investment for other qualifying real property.

"It's not a magic elimination," Jordan said. "It's a deferral. But deferral is a form of wealth if you reinvest wisely."

Example: Alex Buys a Duplex

Alex ran the numbers on a small duplex.

"The rent is good," Alex said. "But the taxes are what scare me."

Jordan replied, "That's why you model depreciation, potential cost seg, your passive loss position, and your long-term plan. Real estate is not just buying a building. It's buying a tax schedule."

CHAPTER 18

ೞ

Investing Like the Elite:
Opportunity Zones and QSBS Strategies

Alex used to think "elite investing" meant private jets and secret handshakes.

Jordan reframed it: "Elite investing is often just tax-aware investing. Same markets. Different outcomes."

Opportunity Zones: The Old Clock and the New Permanent Program

Under the original Opportunity Zone rules, a taxpayer could generally defer eligible capital gains by investing into a Qualified Opportunity Fund (QOF) within the required time window. But deferred gain under that original system generally becomes taxable no later than December 31, 2026 (or earlier if the QOF investment is disposed of).

The One Big Beautiful Bill Act made Opportunity Zones a permanent program—but with a reset.

Current Opportunity Zone designations sunset at the end of 2026, and new zones are designated on a rolling cycle (generally every ten years), starting with a new designation process that takes effect in 2027.

For investments made after December 31, 2026, the deferral mechanics change: the initial gain can generally be deferred for five years from the date of the investment, with a 10 percent basis increase at the five-year mark. (The old seven-year basis step-up is eliminated for new investments.)

Rural Opportunity Zones receive enhanced benefits: a 30 percent basis increase at year five and a reduced "substantial improvement" threshold in many cases.

"Same concept," Jordan said. "But the calendar matters. The strategy changes depending on whether you're in the old program timeline or the new one."

QSBS: The C-Corp Golden Ticket (Now with a Faster Ramp)

Qualified Small Business Stock (QSBS) can allow eligible taxpayers to exclude gain on the sale of certain C corporation stock if the requirements are met.

Under the updated rules, QSBS acquired after July 4, 2025, has a tiered holding-period benefit: 50 percent gain exclusion after three years, 75 percent after four years, and 100 percent after five years.

The rules also expand the definition of a "qualified small business" for new QSBS: the gross assets test increased to $75,000,000 (from the old $50,000,000) for stock acquired after July 4, 2025.

And the per-issuer gain exclusion cap increased for new QSBS: up to $15,000,000 of eligible gain (or ten times basis, if greater), for stock acquired after July 4, 2025.

"So why doesn't everyone do this?" Alex asked.

"Because it only works if you build the company and structure the stock correctly from the start," Jordan replied. "QSBS is not a last-minute tax trick. It's a formation decision."

Example: Alex Invests Like an Owner, Not a Gambler

Jordan sketched two scenarios: buying stock in a promising C corporation that qualifies as a small business versus buying an LLC interest that will never be QSBS.

"The investment might perform the same," Jordan said. "But the tax outcome can be radically different."

Alex wrote a note in the margin: "Ask about QSBS before I invest, not after I win."

CHAPTER 19

☙

Strategic Giving:
Charitable Trusts, Foundations, and
the Philanthropist's Tax Playbook

Alex had always seen charity as pure generosity. Jordan did not disagree—but Jordan also saw the tax code as a set of levers that could increase impact.

"Giving is still giving," Jordan said. "But starting in 2026, the rules for the deduction change in ways that make planning matter more."

What Changed in 2026 Under the One Big Beautiful Bill Act

Jordan laid out the major 2026 shifts.

1)   A new, above-the-line charitable deduction for non-itemizers: Starting in 2026, taxpayers who take the standard deduction can also deduct cash donations up to $1,000 (single) or $2,000 (married filing jointly). This deduction does not apply to gifts to donor-advised funds and certain private foundations, and it is not indexed for inflation.

2)   A new floor for itemizers: If you itemize, charitable contributions are generally only deductible to the extent they exceed 0.5 percent of your adjusted gross income.

3)   A cap on the tax benefit for top-bracket donors: For

103

taxpayers in the highest bracket, the value of itemized deductions is limited—effectively capping the benefit at 35 percent instead of 37 percent.

4)   Higher cash-gift capacity: The 60 percent of AGI limit for cash contributions to public charities is now permanent, which helps in very high-giving years.

"So the rules are tighter for some donors, but there's a new doorway for everyday givers," Alex summarized.

"Exactly," Jordan said. "Which means strategy depends on which door you walk through: itemizing or not."

Bunching: Turning Small Gifts Into Itemized Years

Jordan explained the classic move: bunch multiple years of charitable giving into one year so you clear the standard deduction and the new 0.5 percent AGI floor, then take the standard deduction in other years.

"It's not changing your generosity," Jordan said. "It's changing your timing."

DAFs, Private Foundations, and Trusts: Still Powerful (But Match the Tool to the Goal)

Donor-advised funds (DAFs) can still be useful for bunching and for organizing long-term giving, even though the new non-itemizer deduction generally does not apply to DAF contributions.

Private foundations and charitable trusts can create even more control and planning flexibility, but they come with complexity, administrative responsibilities, and stricter rules.

Example: Alex Plans a Giving Year

Alex ran a simple test with Jordan.

"If my AGI is $200,000," Alex said, "then the first $1,000 of itemized giving won't count because of the 0.5 percent floor. So I either give enough to get past the floor, or I time gifts so the deduction is worth the paperwork."

Jordan nodded. "Now you're thinking like a strategist. The goal is impact first—and then using the tax rules to stretch that impact."

CHAPTER 20

 C3 80

Entity Engineering:
S-Corps, C-Corps, and
Partnerships for High-Income Tax Planning

A lex had assumed the business structure was just paperwork. Jordan disagreed. "Your entity is a tax lens. It changes how income is taxed, how losses behave, and what strategies are even available."

S Corporation: Salary + Distribution (and Payroll Tax Planning)

In an S corporation, owners who work in the business generally take a reasonable salary (subject to payroll taxes) and can receive additional profits as distributions (generally not subject to self-employment tax).

"The word to remember is reasonable," Jordan said. "If you pay yourself $20,000 to do a $200,000 job, the IRS will not be amused."

S corporations also interact with the qualified business income (QBI) deduction. W-2 wages can matter for higher-income owners, and the wage-and-property limits can turn payroll strategy into QBI strategy.

Partnerships and LLCs: Flexibility (and Complexity)

Partnership taxation offers flexibility in allocations, contributions, and distributions. But it also comes with complexity: basis calculations, special allocations, self-employment tax rules, and more.

"Partnerships are powerful," Jordan said, "but the power comes from the details."

C Corporations: When Double Tax Can Be a Feature

C corporations can be a fit when a business plans to reinvest profits, bring in outside investors, or aim for qualified small business stock (QSBS) treatment.

"If QSBS is on the table," Jordan explained, "a C corporation may be the only structure that makes the strategy possible."

How OBBBA Makes Entity Choice More Strategic

Jordan summarized the 2026-era connections:

- QBI is permanent, so pass-through planning has a longer runway.
- One hundred percent bonus depreciation is permanent for qualifying property, which can amplify depreciation-driven strategies.
- Section 179 limits are higher, making expensing easier for growing businesses.
- QSBS is more flexible for new stock with a tiered holding-period exclusion and higher caps.

"So what do I pick?" Alex asked.

Jordan answered like a planner, not a salesman: "We pick the entity that fits your income, your growth plan, your investors, and your exit. The best entity is the one that matches your real business story."

APPENDIX A

෫෨

Year-Round Tax Planning Checklist

Use this checklist to stay proactive throughout the year. Adapt it to your filing status, income type (W-2, 1099, business, rentals), and any major life events.

Quick Start: Your Annual "Tax Snapshot" (Fifteen Minutes)

Do this once at the start of each calendar year (or anytime you decide to get serious about planning).

- Pull last year's filed return (Form 1040 + schedules). Keep it as your baseline.
- Create a "Tax Folder" for the current year (digital and/or paper).
- Confirm your filing status and dependents for the year ahead.
- Review your W-4 withholding (or estimated tax approach if self-employed).
- List your income streams: W-2, 1099, business, rental, investment, retirement, and so on.
- List your major planned moves: home purchase/sale, job change, new business, relocation, marriage/divorce, new child, large medical spend, charitable gifts.
- Set up "capture systems": receipt app, mileage log,

and a place to save statements and confirmations.

Quarterly Checklist (Repeat Every Three Months)

Q1: January through March
- Gather tax documents as they arrive (W-2, 1099s, mortgage interest statements, brokerage statements).
- If you have a side business, open or confirm a separate bank account and start clean bookkeeping.
- Start or continue a mileage log if you use a vehicle for business or other deductible travel.
- If you expect to owe tax outside W-2 withholding, plan (or update) estimated payments with a professional.

Q2: April through June
- After filing, note what moved your tax bill most (deductions, credits, business expenses).
- Adjust withholding or estimated payments based on the filed return's results.
- Review retirement and HSA contribution targets and set an automatic contribution plan if possible.

Q3: July through September
- Midyear check: compare year-to-date income versus last year (raises, bonuses, new contracts).
- If self-employed, confirm you are tracking income and expenses monthly (not annually).
- Plan any major business purchases or upgrades with documentation in mind (date placed in service, business use, receipts).

Q4: October through December
- Run a year-end projection: expected total income, withholding, and likely deductions.
- Time any deductible spending or charitable giving (as appropriate) to match your tax picture.

- Confirm retirement, HSA, and other contribution deadlines and required documentation.

Before You Buy or Commit: "Deduction Reality Check"

Before large purchases or big financial moves, ask:

- Is this personal or business (or mixed)? If mixed, how will I document the business use percentage?
- What proof will I have (receipt + payment record + business purpose)?
- Does timing matter (this year versus next year)?
- Does it interact with another rule (phaseouts, limits, alternative minimum tax, passive loss rules)?

Life Events That Should Trigger a Tax Check-In

- Marriage, divorce, or separation.
- New child, adoption, or a dependent moving in/out.
- Job change, major raise, severance, or large bonus.
- Starting a business, taking on a partner, or changing entity type.
- Buying/selling a home, refinancing, or moving states.
- Selling a business, major stock sale, or exercising stock options.
- Major medical expenses, disability, or caregiving responsibilities.
- Charitable giving plans (especially large gifts or bunching strategies).

Tax Season Checklist (January through April)

- Reconcile your income documents to bank deposits and payroll records.
- Confirm your documentation is complete for any large deductions (home office, travel, meals, vehicle,

charity, medical).
- Double-check the "new and temporary" deductions and credits for the year and keep proof of eligibility.
- If you used a professional, bring: prior return, year summary, and your organized logs (not a shoebox).

Reminder: This checklist is educational. Tax rules change, and outcomes depend on facts. When in doubt, consult a qualified tax professional.

APPENDIX B

 C3&D

Documentation and Recordkeeping Toolkit

U se these templates and checklists to document deductions. Strong records convert "maybe" deductions into defensible deductions.

Audit-Ready Documentation: The Three-Part Proof Test

For most deductions, aim to keep three categories of proof:
- Proof of payment (bank/credit card statement, canceled check, receipt showing paid).
- Proof of what you bought (itemized receipt or invoice).
- Proof of the business purpose or eligibility (a note, calendar entry, contract, or written explanation).

Suggested Digital Folder Structure

1) Income (W-2, 1099, K-1, statements)
2) Deductions—itemized (SALT, mortgage interest, charity, medical)
3) Deductions—adjustments (HSA, IRA, student loan interest, educator)
4) Business (Schedule C): income, expenses, mileage, assets
5) Real estate (Schedule E): income/expenses, depreciation records

6) Credits (child/family/education/energy, if applicable)
7) Withholding and estimated payments
8) Tax prep (drafts, organizer, filed return, correspondence)

Common Retention Guidance (General)

Retention rules depend on your facts. The following is a list of common practices:

- Keep filed returns and supporting documents for at least three years after filing.
- Keep certain items longer (for example, when substantial underreporting, loss claims, or basis in property is involved).
- Keep proof of basis for assets (home improvements, investment purchases) as long as you own the asset, plus the period after sale.

When in doubt, keep it longer—or confirm a retention plan with your tax professional.

Templates

Mileage Log (Vehicle Use)

Use one line per trip. Record mileage contemporaneously when possible.
- Date:
- Start location →End location:
- Business purpose:
- Odometer start / odometer end (or miles driven):
- Total miles for trip:
- Notes (tolls, parking, client name):

Business Expense Log (General)
- Date:

- Vendor / payee:
- Category (supplies, software, advertising, etc.):
- Amount:
- Payment method:
- Receipt file name/link:
- Business purpose note:

Meals Log (Business Meals)
- Date and location:
- Attendees and business relationship:
- Business purpose (what was discussed and why it was necessary):
- Amount and payment method:
- Receipt saved (Yes/No):

Travel Log (Overnight Business Travel)
- Destination and dates:
- Business purpose:
- Transportation (airfare/rail/car):
- Lodging:
- Meals:
- Other (conference fees, taxis, baggage, etc.):
- Receipts saved (Yes/No):

Home Office Worksheet (If Applicable)
Home office deductions are documentation-heavy. Track the following:
- Office square footage:
- Total home square footage:
- Business-use percentage (office ÷ total):
- Direct office expenses (repairs in office only):
- Indirect expenses (utilities, insurance, rent/mortgage interest, property tax, repairs):
- Exclusive and regular use statement (keep a short written note):

Charitable Donation Checklist

- Charity name and EIN (if available):
- Date and method of donation:
- Cash amount or description of property donated:
- Written acknowledgment saved (especially for larger gifts):
- For non-cash gifts, how value was determined and any required forms:

Medical Expense Tracker (If Itemizing)

- Provider:
- Date of service:
- Type of expense (visit, prescription, equipment, etc.):
- Amount paid out-of-pocket:
- Reimbursed by insurance/HSA/FSA (Yes/No):
- Receipt/explanation of benefits (EOB) saved (Yes/No):

Depreciable Asset Purchase Log (Business Equipment)

- Asset description:
- Date purchased:
- Date placed in service:
- Cost (including tax/shipping):
- Business-use percentage (if mixed use):
- Invoice/receipt saved (Y/N):

Tip: If you want your future self to thank you, write a one-sentence "why this qualifies" note the same day you save the receipt.

APPENDIX C

ᢒ᠍ᢇ

Forms, Schedules, and Where Things Go

This appendix is a roadmap for where common items typically appear on US federal tax forms. Forms and lines can change year to year—always follow the current IRS instructions or your tax software prompts.

Core Forms and Schedules

- Form 1040 (main individual return).
- Schedule 1 (additional income and adjustments to income).
- Schedule A (itemized deductions).
- Schedule C (profit or loss from business, sole proprietor).
- Schedule E (rental real estate and pass-through income, if applicable).
- Schedule 3 (credits and other payments, if applicable).

Where Common Deductions Usually "Live" (High-Level)

- Standard deduction: Form 1040 (standard deduction section).
- Itemized deductions (SALT, mortgage interest, charitable, medical): Schedule A.

- Above-the-line adjustments (HSA, IRA deduction, student loan interest, educator expenses): typically Schedule 1.
- Self-employment business expenses: Schedule C.
- Depreciation and Section 179: Form 4562 (often flows to Schedule C or E).
- Home office: Form 8829 (if required) flowing to Schedule C.
- Rental income/expenses and depreciation: Schedule E (and Form 4562 as needed).

Document Checklist by Topic (What to Gather)

SALT (State and Local Taxes)
- Property tax bills and proof of payment.
- State income tax withholding (W-2) and/or estimated payment confirmations.

Mortgage Interest and Property Taxes
- Mortgage interest statement(s) and year-end escrow summary (if applicable).
- Closing statement for purchases/refinances.

Charitable Contributions
- Receipts/acknowledgment letters, donation confirmations, and contemporaneous records.

Medical Expenses (If Itemizing)
- Receipts, invoices, and insurance explanation of benefits (EOBs) to track out-of-pocket amounts.

Side Business Expenses
- Income records (invoices, payment processor reports) and bank deposits.
- Receipts and logs for major categories (supplies,

software, advertising, home office, travel, meals).
- Mileage log and vehicle records if claiming vehicle-related deductions.

Special Note on New or Temporary Deductions

When Congress adds a new deduction (for example, deductions tied to tips, overtime, or auto loan interest), the IRS may implement it as a new line, a worksheet, or an adjustment entry within existing schedules. Follow the IRS instructions for that tax year and retain proof of eligibility and calculation.

For statute, regulation, publication, and case references, see the Table of Authorities.

TABLE OF AUTHORITIES

I. Statutes (Internal Revenue Code)

(Listed numerically)
IRC § 1
IRC § 24
IRC § 62
IRC § 63
IRC § 67(g)
IRC § 68
IRC § 121
IRC § 151
IRC § 162
IRC § 163(h)
IRC § 164
IRC § 168
IRC § 170
IRC § 179
IRC § 199A
IRC § 213
IRC § 221
IRC § 223
IRC § 274
IRC § 280A
IRC § 401(k)
IRC § 403(b)
IRC § 408
IRC § 409A
IRC § 415
IRC § 469

IRC § 664
IRC § 1031
IRC § 1202
IRC § 1400Z-2
IRC §§ 4940–4945

II. Treasury Regulations

Treasury Regulation § 1.63-1
Treasury Regulation § 1.163-10T
Treasury Regulation § 1.170A-13
Treasury Regulation § 1.199A-1 through -6
Treasury Regulation § 1.274-5
Treasury Regulation § 1.280A-2
Treasury Regulation § 1.469-9
Treasury Regulation § 1.1400Z2

III. IRS Publications and Guidance

IRS Publication 463 (Travel, Gift, and Car Expenses)
IRS Publication 502 (Medical and Dental Expenses)
IRS Publication 526 (Charitable Contributions)
IRS Publication 587 (Business Use of Your Home)
IRS Publication 936 (Home Mortgage Interest Deduction)
IRS Publication 946 (How to Depreciate Property)
IRS Publication 969 (HSAs and Other Tax-Favored Health Plans)
IRS Publication 970 (Tax Benefits for Education)
IRS Notice 2020-75 (PTE SALT workaround)
IRS annual inflation adjustment revenue procedure (e.g., Revenue Procedure 2025-32 for 2026 figures)

IV. Case Law

Atkinson v. Commissioner, 115 T.C. 26 (2000).
Commissioner v. Soliman, 506 US 168 (1993).
Hernandez v. Commissioner, 490 US 680 (1989).
Miller v. Commissioner, 243 F.2d 883 (5th Cir. 1957).

About the Author

Brian T. Boyd, Esq., is the author of *Turn Tax Deductions into Wealth - Legal Tax Strategies for W-2 Earners and Entrepreneurs.*

This book was written to help everyday taxpayers understand how US federal income tax rules—especially deductions—can influence real-world financial outcomes.

The examples in this book are educational and illustrative. Tax rules can change, and how they apply depends on individual facts and circumstances.

For personal tax advice, readers should consult a qualified tax professional.